GLUTEN-FREE AND VEGAN

Holidays

GLUTEN-FREE AND VEGAN

Holidays

Celebrating the Year with Simple,
Satisfying Recipes and Menus

JENNIFER KATZINGER

Author of *Flying Apron's Gluten-Free & Vegan Baking Book*

SASQUATCH BOOKS
SEATTLE

Printed in China
Published by Sasquatch Books
Distributed by PGW/Perseus
17 16 15 14 13 12 11   9 8 7 6 5 4 3 2 1

Cover photograph: Kathryn Barnard
Cover design: Anna Goldstein
Interior photographs: Kathryn Barnard
Food styling: Patty Wittmann
Interior design: Anna Goldstein and Rosebud Eustace
Interior composition: Anna Goldstein
Interior illustrations: Clipart.com/ 2011 © Jupiterimages Corporation

Library of Congress Cataloging-in-Publication Data is available.

ISBN-13: 978-1-57061-696-9
ISBN-10: 1-57061-696-5

Sasquatch Books
119 South Main Street, Suite 400
Seattle, WA 98104
(206) 467-4300
www.sasquatchbooks.com
custserv@sasquatchbooks.com

For my daughter,
Lillian Frances

Contents

RECIPE LIST

Fourth of July

Halloween

Birthday Cakes

Acknowledgments

AUTHORING A SECOND COOKBOOK is a dream come true! There are so many family members, friends, and colleagues who have nourished within me the courage to follow this path of creative expression that is in such harmony with my sense of purpose and joy.

Thank you Joseph. Every step I take in diving into a new project I take surrounded with the absoluteness of your tenderness, strength, and love. It is because of us that my greatest dreams have come true. Thank you Lilli. Your wisdom, purity, and enthusiasm for great and small inspire me to stretch every day to try out a new perspective. It is my greatest privilege to be your mommy.

Thank you Jules and Andy. You both have encouraged me to follow my heart. That encouragement has been key at such pivotal moments and has provided the space for another cookbook to be written. Thank you Mom for always being a culinary influence and for your beautiful, loving heart. Thank you Malcolm for your guidance, respect, constant openheartedness, and love. Thank you Kathy for your abundant support, friendship, love, and honesty. Thank you Dad for forever being such a source of strength and love and for the example you give in following one's heart. Thank you Jer, Leon, Josh, Sherri, and Caleb for your enthusiasm and family blessings. Thank you Gabriel! Your friendship is profound!

Many thanks to Susan Roxborough for the opportunity, trust, and guidance in creating this delicious book! Thank you Rachelle Longé for being such a graceful and wonderful editor. Even your e-mails feel like they come from the hand of an artist. Thank you Diane Sepanski for your ever-so-helpful insights. Many thanks to Kathryn Barnard, whose artistry has truly made this book come to life with such vibrancy. Thank you ever so much Patty Wittmann—your finesse and beautiful style shines in each photograph. Thank you Tess Tabor for your constant enthusiasm. Thank you Anna Goldstein—your design expertise will no doubt help each reader follow the recipes with ease. Thank you to everyone at Sasquatch Books who has brought this project to life. It really is a dream come true being able to write cookbooks with such a respected and capable publishing company.

INTRODUCTION

HOLIDAYS FOR ME ARE FILLED WITH expectations, merriment, joy, fuss, and juggling. There is a rather strong side of me that rises up every year and says, "Skip it!" That says I should keep it simple—why spend so much energy running around trying to please a number of people when my own soul is craving quiet peace? Why not travel to some beautiful, warm island for the winter holiday season and reemerge when the whole hullabaloo is over? So when Sasquatch Books asked me to do another gluten-free and vegan cookbook, I was absolutely thrilled, but when the subject was to be holiday cooking, I had to face an internal dilemma. I had to resolve the conundrum of my own confused view of the holidays, and I wanted to have authenticity while authoring this cookbook, both for myself and for all of you who are excited by these recipes.

During my childhood, holidays were indeed magical. However, some-where in my early adulthood a shift took place. Perhaps it was due to my growing awareness of the consumerism and materialism that pervade and overwhelm the holiday seasons as well as the lack of fairly traded and envi-ronmentally responsible products. At the same time this new perspective was taking hold, my family was spreading out around the globe, and so it became a physical challenge for all of us to be together for the holidays. While feeling less and less of a connection to the holiday magic I once experienced, I also happened to meet and marry a wonderful man who grew up celebrating holidays I knew very little about. My husband shared a similar disconnect from the holidays, and yet he was also grateful for his traditions and memories. This left us both somewhat confused about how to move forward, especially as new parents. We both know that we want to create rich, spiritual, magical, and joyful traditions. Do we create new holidays? How do we draw from both of our traditions and make the holidays a reflection of our values, gratitude, and joy? While we are still finding our way, elements of our new path are becoming clearer. One thing that stands out more than anything else for us is that holidays are meant to be spent with people you love, celebrating life together; taking time to stop and appreciate, reflect, give thanks; and sharing merriment, laughter, and beautiful food.

While my husband grew up celebrating traditional Jewish holidays, I grew up celebrating traditional Christian ones. In writing this cookbook and creating gluten-free, vegan recipes that reflect and are inspired by the traditional foods and menus these two cultures celebrate, I am indeed in a wonderful culinary and cultural position: my marriage has allowed me to learn firsthand about traditions previously unfamiliar to me. In these first years of my daughter's life, I have been undertaking delicious experiments in the pursuit of developing this holiday celebrations cookbook. As I create culinary traditions for my own family, I share the best ones with you.

Since the release of my first cookbook, *Flying Apron's Gluten-Free & Vegan Baking Book*, and the birth of my daughter, Lilli, I have sold the Flying Apron Bakery. Embarking on this new chapter in life and being able to jump into the ever-so-new waters of motherhood with my undivided attention is an incredible gift. While diving into the unfamiliar territory of being a parent and no longer a bakery owner, I have taken with me my passion for creating unique baked goods, entrées, flavors, and textures.

Compared to almost a decade ago when I was developing recipes for the bakery's opening, the variety of readily available gluten-free grains has substantially increased. It is so exciting to be working with flours such as coconut, teff, sorghum, almond meal, and hazelnut! I am also delighted to experiment with chia seeds, which, after soaking, work beautifully as a binder. Another newer ingredient to me is coconut oil, and I have been having delicious results with it in many of my new recipes. In bringing you these new recipes, I have maintained my commitment to using unrefined flours, wholesome sweeteners, and healthy fats. The recipes also continue to be soy-free, and many contain less sugar than standard baked goods.

For each holiday you will find a complete menu with accompanying recipes. Although some traditional dishes—such as mashed potatoes, cranberry relish, and charoset—are perhaps easy enough to create from scratch as gluten-free and vegan offerings without the help of a cookbook, I wanted to offer readers a full menu for each holiday. I felt it would be more enticing, convenient, and exciting to provide a complete set of recipes with both the standard classics and the fresh newcomers equally welcome at the table. Note that most of the menus serve four to six people, but all of the recipes in this book are easily doubled or halved.

May these recipes become part of your family's traditions as they have ours. Wishing you the happiest holidays, success in the kitchen, and merriment at your table!

About the Recipes

LIKE THE RECIPES IN MY FIRST BOOK, the ones you'll find here probably look different from those found in other vegan or gluten-free cookbooks. Some of the characteristics that make the recipes in this collection unique and well adapted for a variety of celebrations are detailed here.

Soy-Free, Dairy-Free, and Egg-Free

All of the recipes in this book are gluten-free, plant-based, and made from whole foods. So that they can be enjoyed by all, the recipes are also very allergy friendly: they are soy-free, dairy-free, and egg-free—a rare combination.

I've noticed over the years that many vegan cookbooks depend heavily on soy as a substitute for eggs and milk. While soy is a wonderfully nutritious food, there are many people who suffer from soy allergies, so its use is omitted here. Aside from being less allergenic, soy-, dairy-, and egg-free foods have the added bonus of being cholesterol-free. I've received a lot of positive feedback from people who have really appreciated the absence of soy in my recipes.

Whole Grains and Local, Organic Products

Many gluten-free recipes rely heavily on refined flours and starches, such as tapioca starch, potato starch, eggs, egg replacement products, and white rice flour. You will notice that the flours used in these recipes are all made with whole grains. Given the health benefits of whole grains, I strongly prefer their use over processed and refined flours and starches. In addition, the oils suggested in this cookbook are pure, organic, and cold pressed, and the majority are low in saturated fats.

The sweeteners used in many cookbooks tend to be refined and unhealthy. Instead of those, the recipes that follow utilize natural sweeteners such as maple syrup, Sucanat, date sugar, molasses, agave syrup, and powdered evaporated cane juice.

Michael Pollan (*Food Rules, In Defense of Food*) emphasizes the importance of using as many local ingredients as possible, and I would like to encourage the same. Of course, "local" ingredients vary from one place to another; I welcome you to modify these recipes to adapt to the local options that are available to you.

Finally, note that none of the recipes call specifically for organic ingredients. That said, I do enthusiastically encourage you to choose organic ingredients whenever possible. When you choose organic ingredients, you are selecting foodstuffs free from harmful pesticides as well as pulled from a richer soil, which in turn provides more minerals and nutrients for our bodies. You are supporting sustainable farming methods that protect and enhance the microorganisms and biodiversity of the soil and the surrounding ecosystems. And the farmhands working on organic farms are safe from exposure to the carcinogenic pesticides so abundantly used on nonorganic farms.

Finding Special Ingredients

If you have celiac disease or are gluten-intolerant, it's a good idea to consistently check that the sources of your ingredients are safe from gluten contamination. There are some very trustworthy brands such as Bob's Red Mill and Lundberg, for example. Some companies that sell brown rice flour, bean flours, oats, or other would-be gluten-free ingredients mill where other gluten grains are milled, making what should be a gluten-free ingredient a carrier of gluten. Thankfully, awareness of gluten intolerance has grown so tremendously that buying gluten-free ingredients has become increasingly easy over the years. Check with the Gluten Intolerance Group (www.gluten .net) for sources of gluten-free ingredients near you.

Some of the ingredients in this cookbook may require a trip to a specialty store or may need to be ordered online. Others are common enough to be shelved in the health food section of large grocery stores. Here are a few of note:

Agave syrup comes from the agave plant. The plant is crushed in order to extract a juicy sap, which is heated to create the sweet agave syrup. This syrup is unusual in that it is primarily fructose. There is much debate over agave syrup being considered a healthy choice because of the processing it undergoes to change the molecular structure for sweetness. However, since it is mostly fructose, this sweetener has a low glycemic index, which is appealing to many.

Almond meal is made from ground sweet almonds and has a consistency much like cornmeal. Almond meal adds moistness and a rich nutty taste to baked goods.

Amaranth flour has a very distinct and delightfully unusual flavor. This flour is wonderfully high in fiber and protein.

Arrowroot powder is a unique starch in that it contains calcium ash and trace sea minerals. It has a lovely, fine, powdery consistency that lends lightness to baked goods. It is also a wonderful thickener for sauces and gravies. Surprisingly, arrowroot powder is very unrefined: the arrowroot is simply dried and powdered to make the flour.

Brown rice flour is an excellent source of fiber. It contains some protein and significant amounts of the minerals selenium and magnesium. Brown rice flour has a very delicate flavor.

Buckwheat flour has a distinctive and particularly hearty taste. Buckwheat is actually a flower. When milled, it makes a beautiful dark-hued flour. Buckwheat is very easily digested and is close to being a complete protein in that it contains all eight essential amino acids. It is also high in fiber as well as B vitamins.

Chia seeds are a member of the mint family. What is so remarkable about them is that when they are left to soak in water, they transform into a very thick gelatin. Chia seeds are a fantastic source of soluble fiber, and they help to slow down the conversion of carbohydrates into sugar while in the stomach. They are also a source of omega-3 fatty acids. They are very healthful and act as a binding agent in many of the gluten-free doughs.

Coconut flour is made from the fiber of coconut meat after its oil has been extracted. This flour is high in fiber and protein, adds body to baked goods, and tastes slightly sweet.

Coconut oil is extracted from coconut meat. I particularly like to use coconut oil for frostings because it has such a wonderfully smooth consistency. It works beautifully for pie and tart crusts because of its high melting point. Something interesting to note about coconut oil is that it contains large amounts of lauric acid, a rare medium-chain fatty acid found in breast milk that supports healthy metabolism.

Date sugar is an unprocessed sugar made from dehydrated dates that are ground into small bits. Date sugar is high in fiber, and contains many vitamins and minerals, including iron.

Evaporated cane juice comes from sugar cane like refined sugar; however, evaporated cane juice is processed to a much lesser degree. Because of this, it retains more of the nutrients found in sugar cane. **Powdered evaporated cane juice** is evaporated cane juice that has been ground to an extremely fine powder with the addition of a small amount of cornstarch. The unrefined powdered evaporated cane juice retains some of the sugar cane's molasses as well as some vitamins and minerals.

Forbidden rice is a type of heirloom rice that has a gorgeous black color due to its coating of black bran. This bran adds nutritional value as well as complexity to the rice's flavor. Forbidden rice is high in fiber, antioxidants, iron, and other trace minerals.

Garbanzo bean flour can be a great choice for adding more substance to gluten-free doughs. It has a delightful earthy flavor. Garbanzo bean flour is high in protein, fiber, and iron.

Hazelnut flour is a slightly sweet and nutty flour that adds great texture and exceptional flavor to baked goods. Hazelnuts and hazelnut flour are rich in vitamin E as well as potassium and magnesium.

Quinoa flour is made from ground quinoa seeds. This unique flour has a mild, nutty, and addictive taste. It is one of the most nutritious flours one could possibly use. Quinoa flour has more protein than any other flour and is high in zinc, iron, calcium, vitamin B, phosphorus, potassium, magnesium, and manganese. I use quinoa mainly in savory dishes and baked goods.

Sorghum flour comes from the whole grain kernel of sorghum. Nutritionally, sorghum is much like corn, but higher in protein and fat. It has a very mellow taste and is quite enjoyable in baked goods.

Sucanat is made from the whole sugar cane and is a type of evaporated cane juice. All evaporated cane juices are made by extracting juice from the sugar cane and boiling the juice to remove water. Sucanat is unique because the syrup leftover after boiling the cane juice is actually hand paddled to be cooled and dried. Sucanat retains all of the sugar cane and molasses, making it the most nutritious of all the sugar cane sweeteners.

Teff flour is milled from the whole grain teff. As it so happens, teff is the world's smallest whole grain. Teff flour has a delightful, wholesome, yet mellow taste. The protein content of teff flour is exceptional in that it contains all eight essential amino acids. Teff flour is also abundant in fiber, calcium, copper, and iron.

Xanthan gum is used to add elasticity to gluten-free doughs. Xanthan gum is a natural product that is usually a result of the fermentation of corn, but can also be derived from other plant matter. This process of fermentation is similar to the fermentation of beer, cheese, and yogurt.

Gluten-Free Baking versus Traditional Baking

Cooks and bakers accustomed to traditional baking may find gluten-free baking much different than what they are used to. If you are new to gluten-free baking, I strongly advise you to read through and study an entire recipe before starting, and to take care when shaping baked goods and checking for doneness. This may take some experimentation, but with a little bit of practice you will gain familiarity with how the doughs should feel.

Because these gluten-free breads are made with unrefined flours and do not include starch binders such as tapioca or potato, you will find that it is important to not overmix or overknead your dough. As soon as the loaves are shaped, the dough must go directly into the hot oven. The goal is to capture the gases of the yeast as the bread bakes rather than as the bread rises outside of the oven. Because we want to take advantage of the yeast expanding as the bread bakes, the temperature of the water used to activate the yeast is actually lukewarm, cooler than that of traditional wheat bread recipes. The gases that are released when baking create small air pockets in the bread, giving it the light texture that is found in traditional wheat bread.

A Note about Honey

Honey is an ingredient that many vegans avoid. If you are preparing a recipe that uses honey, be sure to find out if any vegans you're serving object to consuming it. All of the recipes in this book that call for honey also provide an alternative sweetener that can work as a substitute.

GLUTEN-FREE AND VEGAN

Holidays

MENU

....

Autumn Spinach Salad

Acorn Squash with Porcini Mushroom Filling

Herbed Fresh Bread Stuffing
with Golden Raisins

Roasted Sweet Potatoes and Red Onions

Brussels Sprouts with Sautéed Shallots
and Slivered Almonds

Fresh Cranberry Relish

Simple Gravy

Acorn Squash and Sweet Potato Pie

....

SERVES 8

Thanksgiving

THESE RECIPES ARE FULL OF THE FLAVORS OF AUTUMN. During this time of year, with shorter days and a chill in the air, I am grateful for my warm kitchen and the feeling of anticipation of the Thanksgiving feast. Recently, I am finding the winter holidays to be quite valuable, not only because they provide space and time for gathering, but also because I have embraced the creative hustle-and-bustle of the production and planning, in what would otherwise be a rather cold and sleepy time of year.

To spread out the preparations so that Thanksgiving Day isn't spent completely in the kitchen, I have some tips. The acorn squash entrée and filling can be made the day before and assembled and warmed the day it is served. The relish is quite delicious fresh but will hold over beautifully from the day before if kept in an airtight container in the fridge. The pie can also be made the day before, but be sure to warm it before serving.

The day of this gorgeous feast I invite you to engage your guests and family in the remaining meal preparations—it is so enjoyable to create food with others. Your meal will take on an even more fulfilling quality when some of the guests contribute to final touches—and the food may taste even more delectable when made together, with ease and pleasure. Happy Thanksgiving to you!

Autumn Spinach Salad

Having a fresh salad on Thanksgiving is a must for me. Fall spinach is so rich and earthy, and it lends a juicy reminder of the fresh season not so long ago. It really hits the spot with this slightly sweet dressing and the accompaniment of fall fruits and nuts.

1 cup dried cherries

2 cups finely chopped, lightly toasted hazelnuts

3 bunches fresh spinach, leaves washed and dried, torn into bite-size pieces

2 Anjou pears, cored and very thinly sliced

1 small red onion, thinly sliced

¼ cup freshly squeezed orange juice (about 1 medium orange)

3 tablespoons white balsamic vinegar

¾ cup extra-virgin olive oil

1 tablespoon maple syrup

1 teaspoon sea salt

½ teaspoon freshly ground pepper

1. Set aside ½ cup of the cherries and 1 cup of the hazelnuts. Combine the spinach, pears, red onion, and the remaining cherries and hazelnuts in a large mixing bowl. In a small jar or bowl, thoroughly mix the orange juice, vinegar, olive oil, maple syrup, salt, and pepper. Toss the dressing with the salad. For fancy occasions like Thanksgiving, I like to serve this salad equally divided among 8 salad plates, with some reserved cherries and hazelnuts placed atop each as a delicious garnish.

Acorn Squash with Porcini Mushroom Filling

This is indeed an entrée to be grateful for. The porcini mushrooms lend a hearty, rich flavor to the robust filling, which in turn provides a lovely contrast to the soft, sweet squash. The forbidden rice has a delectable nutty flavor and lovely stickiness that is key to this dish. Bon appétit!

4 medium acorn squashes

2 tablespoons plus 2 teaspoons coconut oil

3 cups water

Pinch of sea salt

1 cup forbidden rice (Chinese black rice)

2 medium onions, sliced into very thin half moons

2 vegetable bouillon cubes

6 cloves garlic, minced

4 tomatoes, chopped

3 cups cooked butter beans or lima beans

1 cup dried porcini mushrooms

½ cup finely chopped Italian parsley, for garnish

1. Preheat the oven to 350 degrees F.

2. Begin by halving the squashes and scooping out their seeds. Place 1 teaspoon of the coconut oil in the center of each acorn half, and spread it to coat the inner surfaces. Cover each half with aluminum foil and bake for about 2 hours (depending on the size of your squash), or until the squash is tender when pierced with a fork.

3. While the squash cooks, in a medium saucepan, bring 2 cups of the water to a boil with the salt. Add the rice, reduce the heat, and simmer, covered, for 30 minutes, or until the rice is tender and all the water has been absorbed. Remove from the heat and set aside.

4. While the rice cooks, begin making the filling. In a very large sauté pan, add the onions, remaining 1 cup water, bouillon cubes, and garlic, and bring to a boil over high heat. Reduce the heat to a simmer, then add the reserved rice, tomatoes, beans, and mushrooms. Cover the pan and continue to simmer on low heat for 1½ hours, or until the mixture resembles a thick stew. Divide the filling among the piping-hot acorn squash halves. Garnish each half with a sprinkling of parsley. *Bellissimo!*

Herbed Fresh Bread Stuffing with Golden Raisins

This is a delectable, slightly sweet stuffing. I am a huge fan of fresh herbs and raisins in my stuffing; I know not everyone likes raisins, so if you or your guests object to these sun-dried fruits, feel free to omit them. I recommend making the bread a day or two before your meal, to simplify your time in the kitchen on Thanksgiving Day. A store-bought gluten-free bread or Yam Bread with a Pinch of Magic (page 139) will work with this recipe too, should you find yourself short on time. I should also add that this bread is really terrific on its own. It slices beautifully, has great flavor, and works well as bruschetta, sandwich bread, or simply as toast.

FOR THE BREAD:

¼ cup extra-virgin olive oil

2 tablespoons maple syrup

1½ cups lukewarm water

1 tablespoon active dry yeast

2½ cups teff flour

1 cup brown rice flour, plus extra for kneading the dough

1 teaspoon sea salt

1 teaspoon xanthan gum

FOR THE STUFFING:

5 cups bread crumbs (from recipe above or other gluten-free bread)

¼ cup extra-virgin olive oil, plus extra for oiling the pan and drizzling

4 cloves garlic, minced

2 small onions, chopped

4 ribs celery, finely sliced

2 medium apples, peeled, cored, and chopped

½ cup golden raisins

⅔ cup chopped walnuts

¼ cup minced fresh sage

¼ cup fresh thyme, chopped

1 teaspoon sea salt

1½ cups vegetable broth

Freshly ground pepper

1. To make the bread, preheat the oven to 350 degrees F. Generously dust your work surface with brown rice flour.

2. In a large mixing bowl, combine the olive oil, maple syrup, water, and yeast. In a separate bowl, thoroughly combine the teff and brown rice flours, salt, and xanthan gum.

3. As soon as yeast is active (it will take 3 to 5 minutes), gradually incorporate the dry ingredients into the wet ingredients. This can be done by hand or with an electric mixer on low speed. Mix just until the ingredients are well combined and evenly moist. As soon as the dough has formed, remove it from the bowl; quickly and gently knead it 3 or 4 times on your floured work surface. Divide dough into two pieces, and shape each half into a small baguette. Make a ¼-inch-deep slice down the length of both baguettes. Place them on a baking sheet on the middle rack in the oven and bake for about 1 hour, or until the crust is firm; when the loaves are pierced with a knife, the knife should come out clean. Transfer the baguettes to a rack and let cool. When cool enough to handle, cut the baguettes into small ½-inch cubes. You should have about 5 cups of bread crumbs.

4. To make the stuffing, first preheat the oven to 250 degrees F.

5. Spread the bread cubes on 2 baking sheets and toast for 1 hour, or until they are dry and crisp. Remove them from the oven and let cool. After the cubes have cooled, crush them a little bit with a rolling pin and set aside.

6. Increase the oven temperature to 350 degrees F.

7. Lightly oil a 9-by-13-inch baking pan. In a large sauté pan, add the olive oil. Add the garlic and onions and sauté over low heat until lightly browned, about 10 minutes, and then add the celery and apples. Continue sautéing until the celery and apples have softened slightly, about 10 more minutes. Now toss in the toasted bread crumbs, raisins, walnuts, sage, thyme, and salt. Transfer the stuffing into the prepared baking pan and drizzle in the vegetable broth. Cover the pan with foil and bake for 45 minutes. Remove the foil and drizzle the stuffing with an additional ⅛ cup to ¼ cup olive oil. Leaving the pan uncovered, return it to the oven for 15 more minutes. When you are ready to serve the stuffing, season it to taste with pepper and additional salt.

Roasted Sweet Potatoes and Red Onions

Every Thanksgiving my mother prepares this mouthwatering dish. I love it because it adds a delicious Tuscan flair to our American tradition. The rosemary in particular adds so much brightness, and complements the sweetness of the roasted vegetables and the softness of the roasted garlic, creating a perfect medley of warming flavors.

4 pounds (total) sweet potatoes and yams, peeled and cut into 1-inch cubes

½ cup extra-virgin olive oil

6 garlic cloves, minced

2½ teaspoons sea salt

1½ teaspoons coarsely ground pepper

1½ pounds red onions, halved lengthwise, then cut crosswise into ¼-inch-thick slices

1 tablespoon chopped fresh rosemary

1. Preheat the oven to 375 degrees F. Combine all the ingredients in a large roasting pan. Cook, stirring every 10 minutes, until the potatoes, yams, and onions are tender and brown around the edges, about 1 hour. This dish can be prepared 4 hours ahead of serving. Let stand at room temperature loosely covered with foil. Reheat, uncovered, in a 375-degree oven for about 10 minutes.

Brussels Sprouts with Sautéed Shallots and Slivered Almonds

These earthy, green little gems really mark the fall and winter season for me. A typical Thanksgiving dish I've seen on many tables is green beans with almonds. I couldn't resist offering these delightful miniature cabbages in their place.

2 pounds brussels sprouts, trimmed and halved

3 tablespoons extra-virgin olive oil

2 cups thinly sliced shallots (about 4 medium)

1 cup slivered almonds

1 teaspoon sea salt

2 tablespoons chopped fresh thyme

3 tablespoons snipped fresh chives

Juice of ½ medium lemon (about 1½ tablespoons)

Freshly ground pepper

1. Preheat the oven to 350 degrees F.

2. Heat 2 cups water in a large pan over high heat. Place the brussels sprouts in a steamer basket and steam for 10 to 15 minutes, or until tender. Meanwhile, in a small sauté pan, add the olive oil and sauté the shallots over low heat until they begin to brown, about 10 minutes. While the shallots are cooking, place the almonds in a shallow pan and toast them in the oven until lightly browned, about 7 minutes. In a large serving bowl, gently toss the brussels sprouts, shallots, almonds, salt, thyme, chives, and lemon juice. Season to taste with pepper and additional salt. Serve and enjoy while hot.

Fresh Cranberry Relish

Of course, cranberry relish is meant to be a condiment, but when I created this recipe, I must admit I ate a large bowl of it on its own. I find this relish, with its addition of mint and ginger, to be very refreshing.

1 medium apple, peeled, cored, and chopped

1-inch piece fresh gingerroot, peeled and minced

Zest of 1 medium lemon (about 2 teaspoons)

One 10-ounce bag frozen cranberries

1 cup frozen cherries

Pinch of salt

¼ cup chopped fresh mint

1. This is the simplest of recipes. Place all the ingredients into a food processor and pulse until they are well combined. The texture will be similar to shredded carrots when the relish is ready.

Simple Gravy

This gravy comes together with ease. Just be prepared to whisk continuously for about 10 minutes. Many of us think of gravy as an essential part of the Thanksgiving feast, but it is also delicious on an ordinary day ladled over steamed vegetables, baked potatoes, or your favorite cooked grain. One comfort food I crave on cold days is this simple gravy spooned over hot buckwheat groats.

2 tablespoons garbanzo bean flour

1 tablespoon arrowroot powder

⅓ cup extra-virgin olive oil

1¾ cups vegetable broth

½ teaspoon dried sage

½ teaspoon dried thyme

¼ teaspoon dried marjoram

Sea salt and freshly ground pepper

1. In a small saucepan over low heat combine the garbanzo bean flour, arrowroot powder, and olive oil. Whisk continuously for about 5 minutes to smooth out any lumps and prevent scorching. The gravy will thicken and turn golden. Very slowly add the vegetable broth, continuing to whisk the gravy. Once the broth has been thoroughly incorporated, stir in the sage, thyme, and marjoram. Season to taste with salt and pepper. Serve this delicious gravy warm over stuffing.

Acorn Squash
and Sweet Potato Pie

This is a beautiful pie. The acorn squash lends a floral-like perfume that blends tastily with the warming spices. Pie is always a special treat served à la mode. There are some wonderful alternative, non-dairy ice creams and whipped creams available in many grocery stores that would be a lovely complement to this pie.

FOR THE CRUST:

> ½ cup coconut oil
>
> 1 cup sorghum flour, plus extra for rolling out dough
>
> 1 cup almond meal
>
> 2 tablespoons maple syrup
>
> ½ teaspoon sea salt
>
> 1 tablespoon water

FOR THE FILLING:

> 2 cups cooked acorn squash flesh
>
> 1 cup cooked sweet potato flesh
>
> ¼ teaspoon sea salt
>
> 1 teaspoon ground cinnamon
>
> ½ teaspoon ground nutmeg
>
> ¼ teaspoon ground ginger
>
> 1 teaspoon vanilla extract
>
> ½ cup maple syrup
>
> 2 tablespoons arrowroot powder
>
> ½ cup rice milk

1. To make the pie crust, preheat the oven to 350 degrees F. Generously dust your work surface with sorghum flour.

2. Add all the crust ingredients to the bowl of a food processor and pulse until well combined. Remove the dough and roll it into a 10-inch round, dusting with additional flour as needed. Flip the dough over onto the pie pan. If the crust tears, don't worry—you can mend it by pressing the dough back together with floured hands. For the sides of the pie, I like the dough to be a bit thicker so I can crimp the edges using my thumb and forefinger. Any style will work nicely, though. Chill the pie crust in the freezer for 20 minutes to make the dough sturdier.

3. After the crust has chilled, prebake with pie weights for 20 minutes.

4. To make the filling, combine all the ingredients in the bowl of a stand mixer fitted with the paddle attachment or in a food processor; mix until smooth. Pour the filling into the partially baked crust and bake for an additional 20 minutes, or until the filling appears set but slightly gelatinous. The filling will continue to set up as it cools. Allow the pie to cool slightly before serving.

MENU

Lentil Pâté

Horseradish Beet Salad

Purple Potato Latkes

Spicy Apple Chutney

Homemade Cinnamon Applesauce

Sweet Potato Carrot Kugel

Braided "Challah" Bread (page 62)

Almond Bundt Cake (page 60)

Cookie-Cutter Vanilla Cookies (page 44),
in the shape of dreidels

SERVES 4 TO 6

HANUKKAH

REJOICING IN THE MIRACLE OF LIGHTS, singing songs, lighting the menorah, eating homemade potato latkes—how wonderful! While designing this menu, I did quite a bit of research about what is traditionally served and what flavors play a significant role in the story of Hanukkah. I hope you find this special dinner holds the essence of the traditional fare in a gluten-free, vegan rendition.

To save time I recommend making the lentil pâté, apple chutney, and dreidel cookies the day before. It is also helpful to marinate the beets one day prior to making the salad. The potato pancakes can be formed the day before as well and kept on an aluminum foil–covered plate in the refrigerator; they should be fried right before serving. The braided bread is best made the day it will be served, but the almond bundt cake can be made one day ahead.

Lentil Pâté

*This pâté is festive and scrumptious. The flavor of toasted pecans adds a subtle sweet-
ness that contrasts harmoniously with just the right amount of salty capers. This pâté
is less salty than most (I've left it to the capers to provide most of the salt), but feel free
to season it to your liking. Leftover pâté makes for an excellent sandwich spread: I like
to have mine on toast with avocado and tomato.*

3 cups water

1 cup gray-green lentils

1 bay leaf

4 medium shallots, roughly chopped

1 tablespoon extra-virgin olive oil

1 cup toasted pecans

2 teaspoons chopped fresh thyme

1 tablespoon whole grain mustard

4 tablespoons capers

Sea salt and freshly ground pepper

Thyme sprigs, for garnish

1. In a medium saucepan, add the water, lentils, and bay leaf. Bring to a boil, then
   reduce the heat, cover partially, and simmer for 30 minutes, or until the lentils
   are tender and all the water has been absorbed. While the lentils are cooking,
   in a small skillet, sauté the shallots in the olive oil until soft, about 5 minutes.
   Drain the lentils using a fine-mesh strainer or colander to remove any remaining liquid; remove the bay leaf.

2. In a food processor, combine the lentils, shallots, pecans, thyme, mustard, and 1 tablespoon of the capers. Pulse until the mixture holds together. Fold in the remaining capers and season to taste with salt and pepper. Press the pâté into a bowl and chill until ready to serve. It can be turned out onto a plate and sliced with a knife, or served from the bowl. It is always lovely to garnish this pâté with fresh thyme sprigs.

Horseradish Beet Salad

The sweet, juicy tang of beets, followed by the "Pow!" of horseradish, and a crunch of toasted walnuts over a dressy bed of arugula is my idea of a deliciously powerful salad. Because the beets need to marinate for at least 8 hours or overnight, I recommend starting this recipe the day before serving.

1½ pounds beets, any variety

1½ tablespoons evaporated cane juice

½ cup red wine vinegar

1 tablespoon prepared horseradish

½ teaspoon sea salt

8 ounces fresh arugula or mixed salad greens

½ cup extra-virgin olive oil

Juice of 1 medium lemon (about 3 tablespoons)

Sea salt and freshly ground pepper

1 cup toasted chopped walnuts

1. Bring a large pot of water to a boil, add the beets, and cook until tender, 30 to 45 minutes, depending on the size of your beets. When the beets have cooled, remove their skins and slice them into thin wedges.

2. Meanwhile, prepare the marinade. Combine the evaporated cane juice, red wine vinegar, horseradish, and salt in a large glass bowl. Add the beets, tossing with the marinade to coat them well. Cover and refrigerate overnight or for 8 hours before serving.

3. Right before serving, toss the arugula with the olive oil and lemon juice. Season to taste with salt and pepper. Divide the greens among 4 to 6 salad plates and top with the marinated beets and toasted walnuts.

Purple Potato Latkes

My husband's parents named their first dog Latke. I never had the pleasure of meeting him; however, now that I have thoroughly enjoyed this tasty staple, I understand that he must have been as comforting and pleasing as his namesake. I call for purple potatoes here, but new potatoes or small Yukon Golds work well if purple potatoes are hard to come by in your area. I like to use either my Homemade Cinnamon Applesauce (page 27) or Spicy Apple Chutney (page 26) to complement this dish.

Brown rice flour, for forming the latkes

Canola oil, for frying the latkes

14 small purple potatoes (about 2 pounds)

2 teaspoons sea salt

Freshly ground pepper

½ cup extra-virgin olive oil

1. Lightly dust your work surface with brown rice flour and generously grease a griddle or large sauté pan with canola oil. Scrub the potatoes well, but leave them unpeeled.

2. Set aside half of the potatoes for grating. Slice the remaining potatoes into ½-inch cubes and cook them in a large pot of boiling water until tender, about 20 minutes. Meanwhile, grate the reserved potatoes, then sprinkle with the salt and season to taste with pepper.

3. Drain the cubed potatoes and put them into the bowl of a stand mixer fitted with the paddle attachment. Add the olive oil and mix on low speed until the potatoes are mashed. (Alternatively, you can use a hand mixer or an old-fashioned potato masher to mix the potatoes.) Fold the grated potatoes into

the mashed ones. With floured hands, form this mixture into 16 latkes. Place the latkes on a floured plate. Fry the latkes in batches on the hot griddle until lightly browned, about 3 minutes on each side (longer for a crispier latke). Enjoy hot out of the pan or keep warm in the oven until ready to serve.

Spicy Apple Chutney

My favorite way to enjoy chutney is with potato pancakes hot off the griddle. If you enjoy a more piquant chutney with a kick, double up on the red pepper flakes. This chutney also goes beautifully with Lilli's Spooky, Spicy Garbanzos (page 138) as well as with Quinoa Salt-and-Pepper Crackers (page 33).

1 tablespoon extra-virgin olive oil

1 large onion, minced

¾ teaspoon garam masala

1 pinch red pepper flakes

4 medium apples, peeled, cored, and finely diced

½ cup golden raisins

⅓ cup firmly packed dark brown sugar

¼ cup apple cider vinegar

½ teaspoon grated peeled fresh gingerroot

1. In a medium sauté pan, combine the olive oil, onion, garam masala, and red pepper flakes; sauté over low heat for about 5 minutes, or until the onions are soft. Add the apples, raisins, brown sugar, cider vinegar, and ginger. Let this simmer for an additional 20 minutes, stirring occasionally, until the apples are soft and falling apart. The chutney is delicious served either warm or chilled with potato latkes.

Homemade
Cinnamon Applesauce

Store-bought applesauce doesn't come close to the deliciousness of homemade! This easy recipe makes enough for everyone to have a generous serving with their potato pancakes. Double or even triple this recipe if you want to indulge throughout the week.

2 pounds Braeburn or Fuji apples, peeled, cored, and chopped
    into small chunks
Juice of ½ medium lemon (about 1½ tablespoons)
1 cinnamon stick
Pinch of nutmeg
3 tablespoons Sucanat or evaporated cane juice
½ cup water
Pinch of salt

1. In a medium pot, combine all the ingredients and bring to a boil. Reduce the heat and simmer for 20 minutes, or until the apples are soft. Remove the cinnamon stick, then mash the apples with a fork or potato masher to your desired consistency (I like mine chunky).

Sweet Potato Carrot Kugel

This puddinglike side dish creates quite a seductive aroma as it bakes. Notice your appetite growing as the table is set and wafts of cinnamon from the kitchen draw you in.

3 sweet potatoes (about 1 pound), peeled and grated

1 large apple, cored and grated

1 medium carrot, grated

½ cup golden raisins

½ cup crumbled Gluten-Free Matzo Bread (page 97)

1 teaspoon ground cinnamon

½ cup apple juice

1. Preheat the oven to 350 degrees F. Lightly grease a large 10½-by-7-inch baking dish.

2. In a large mixing bowl, thoroughly combine all the ingredients; press them into the baking dish. Bake for 1 hour, or until crisp on top.

MENU

Quinoa Salt-and-Pepper Crackers
with Almond Cheese

Red Jewel Salad

Stuffed Tomatoes with Basil and
Forbidden Rice

Holiday White Bean Spinach Tart

Twice-Baked Sweet Potatoes

Christmas Fig and Spice Cake with Creamy
Citrus Frosting (page 57)

Assortment of Christmas cookies (see Holiday
Cookies, Cakes, and Breads, page 42)

SERVES 6

Christmas Dinner

THIS MENU INCORPORATES THE TRADITIONAL red and green colors of Christmas. To lighten my load, I prepare the tart dough and fill my tart shells two days before, then freeze them until I'm ready to bake them on Christmas day. The quinoa crackers with almond cheese are delightful and easily prepared a day in advance. (Do note that the almonds need to soak for ten hours before you can make the almond cheese.) I like to serve this appetizer with purchased mixed olives, pickled asparagus spears, and spiced nuts. The sweet potatoes can also be stuffed the day before so that on Christmas they simply need to be reheated. The dessert can be made two days in advance—just be sure to cover your cake with a glass dome or a large bowl to keep it fresh, and store it in a cool, dry spot.

As a final touch, place a baby rosemary plant at each place setting, wrapped at the base with paper and a red bow. It will look festive on the table, and your guests will appreciate this aromatic gift, sure to be used throughout the year.

Quinoa Salt-and-Pepper Crackers with Almond Cheese

The almond cheese is easy to make and tastes like a real indulgence. I developed it to serve with the quinoa crackers, but it also makes a satisfying sandwich spread. If you are pinched for time, of course you can serve this cheese with store-bought gluten-free crackers; however, homemade crackers will make your guests feel special. These quinoa crackers make a satisfying and beautiful prelude to a holiday gathering.

FOR THE QUINOA CRACKERS:

> 1½ cups quinoa flour, plus extra for rolling out dough
>
> ¼ cup coconut oil
>
> ½ cup water
>
> 1 teaspoon baking soda
>
> ½ teaspoon sea salt
>
> ¼ teaspoon freshly ground pepper

FOR THE ALMOND CHEESE:

> 1 cup raw almonds, soaked in water for 10 hours, then drained
>
> ¼ cup chopped fresh thyme leaves, plus extra for garnish
>
> ¼ cup water
>
> ¼ cup extra-virgin olive oil
>
> 2 cloves garlic
>
> ½ teaspoon sea salt
>
> Freshly ground pepper

1. To make the crackers, preheat the oven to 350 degrees F, and lightly dust your work surface and a baking sheet with quinoa flour.

2. Combine all the cracker ingredients in the bowl of a stand mixer fitted with the paddle attachment, and mix thoroughly on low speed. Remove the dough and roll it out on your floured work surface, turning the dough and sprinkling with additional flour as needed to prevent sticking. When the dough is about ⅛ inch thick, cut it into shapes using a cookie cutter or the top of a juice glass. You could instead cut the dough into squares or rectangles using a knife, pizza wheel, or fluted dough wheel.

3. With a spatula, transfer the crackers to the baking sheet, prick each with a fork, and sprinkle with additional salt and pepper. (Alternatively, you could make one large cracker by pressing the dough into a 12-inch tart pan, pricking all over with a fork, and sprinkling with additional salt and pepper.) Bake for 20 minutes. If making one cracker, score it into wedges right when it comes out of the oven. Let the crackers cool for 1 hour before storing on a covered plate or in a cookie tin.

4. To make the cheese, combine all the ingredients except for the pepper in a food processor. Process until the cheese has attained a smooth, creamy texture. Season to taste with the pepper and additional salt. Place the cheese into a mold or bowl and chill until ready to serve. Turn cheese out onto a serving plate and garnish with fresh thyme. (Alternatively, you can form the cheese into individual balls and place one on each quinoa cracker wedge, garnished with fresh thyme.)

Red Jewel Salad

This is a simple salad to accompany the more complex entrées and side dishes. The pomegranate seeds are like little glistening ornaments themselves. Walnut and other nut oils are a lovely addition to any pantry; they provide an earthy, toasty, and rich flavor to dishes and a new dimension to salads such as this one.

10 cups mixed salad greens

Seeds from 2 medium pomegranates (about 1½ cups)

1 cup walnuts, toasted and chopped

1 small red onion, sliced very thinly into half moons

¼ cup balsamic vinegar

¼ cup extra-virgin olive oil

¼ cup walnut oil

½ teaspoon sea salt

Freshly ground pepper

1. In a large bowl, toss all the ingredients together and serve immediately.

Stuffed Tomatoes with Basil and Forbidden Rice

These tomatoes bring holiday cheer to the table with their bright red and green colors. A juicy, warm, sweet tomato stuffed with rice full of rich, savory flavor and abundant with fresh herbs is such a Christmas treat! Although tomatoes aren't in season in the winter, I've purchased hothouse tomatoes that really sweeten up when baked.

1½ cups water

¾ cup forbidden rice (Chinese black rice)

3 tablespoons extra-virgin olive oil

1½ large onions, minced

4 cloves garlic, minced

6 large red slicing tomatoes

⅓ cup chopped fresh basil

1½ tablespoons chopped fresh oregano

2 teaspoons chopped fresh thyme

¾ teaspoon sea salt

Freshly ground pepper

½ cup chopped Italian parsley, for garnish

1. Preheat the oven to 350 degrees F.

2. In a small saucepan, bring the water to a boil and add the rice. Reduce the heat to maintain a simmer and cover. Cook for about 30 minutes, or until all the water has been absorbed.

3. While the rice cooks, heat the olive oil in a large skillet over low heat; sauté the onions and garlic until the onions are transparent and just beginning to brown,

about 10 minutes. Slice the tops off the tomatoes and carefully scoop out the flesh with a small spoon, reserving the shells. Chop the tomato flesh into small pieces and add it to the skillet with the onions and garlic. Add the basil, oregano, thyme, and salt. Simmer for about 20 minutes to meld the flavors and release the tomatoes' juices. Add the cooked rice, mix well, and season to taste with pepper and additional salt.

4. Stuff the reserved tomato shells with this marvelous filling and place them in a large baking dish. Bake, uncovered, for 25 minutes. Serve hot, garnished with the parsley.

Holiday White Bean Spinach Tart

Your guests are in for an unforgettable treat. This tart's Italian flavors begin to entice you as the aroma of rosemary and thyme wafts through the kitchen. Next comes the smell of onions sautéing in olive oil and pine nuts toasting. Do you get the idea? Your tart crust will hold up beautifully with any filling—even a rich, creamy one—while remaining tender and flaky.

FOR THE CRUST:

    1¼ cups brown rice flour

    ¾ cup teff flour

    ½ teaspoon sea salt

    1 teaspoon dried rosemary

    ¼ cup coconut oil

    ¼ cup extra-virgin olive oil

    3 tablespoons water

    ¼ cup finely chopped toasted pine nuts

FOR THE FILLING:

    1 medium onion, sliced thinly into half moons

    2 tablespoons extra-virgin olive oil

    2½ cups cooked butter beans

    ½ teaspoon dried thyme leaves

    1 teaspoon sea salt

    Freshly ground pepper

    2 bunches fresh spinach, washed and drained

1. To make the tart crust, first preheat the oven to 350 degrees F.

2. In a food processor, combine the brown rice and teff flours, salt, and rosemary. Add the coconut oil and olive oil, and pulse until small pearls of dough form. Add the water by tablespoons just until the dough holds together. Fold in the pine nuts. Press the dough into a 10-inch tart pan or divide into 6 equal portions and press each portion into a 3-inch tart pan. Really use your hands to work the dough, creating a thin bottom crust, while forming more substantial sides. Prick the bottom crust(s) with a fork; prebake the 10-inch crust for 15 minutes and the individual crusts for just under 10 minutes.

3. While the crust is baking, begin making the filling. In a large skillet, sauté the onion in the olive oil until it just begins to brown, about 10 minutes. Add the beans, thyme, salt, and pepper to taste. Let this cook for about 5 minutes. Stir in the spinach and remove the pan from the heat. Spoon the filling into the prebaked tart shell(s) and return the tarts to the oven for an additional 7 to 10 minutes, or until piping hot. If you are using a tart pan with a removable bottom, it is best to serve the tart on the bottom layer of the pan, removing the outer ring only. Serve hot.

Twice-Baked Sweet Potatoes

My mouth waters when I smell these baking in my oven. Dinner is about to be served, and I know it's going to be a delicious, joy-filled evening. Rosemary, sage, pecans, and sweet potatoes: what a melody!

6 sweet potatoes (about 2 pounds)

1 teaspoon dried rosemary

1½ teaspoons dried sage

1 teaspoon sea salt

3 tablespoons extra-virgin olive oil

⅔ cup almond milk

¾ cup pecans, lightly toasted and chopped

1. Preheat the oven to 350 degrees F.

2. Thoroughly scrub the sweet potatoes. Place them on a cookie sheet and bake for 1 hour, or until the potatoes are soft and cooked through. Set aside until the potatoes are cool enough to handle.

3. Slice the potatoes lengthwise along the top. With a spoon, gently scoop out the flesh of each potato. In a food processor or the bowl of a stand mixer fitted with the paddle attachment, combine the sweet potato flesh, rosemary, sage, salt, olive oil, and almond milk. Process until the mixture attains a smooth consistency.

4. Scoop this filling back into each sweet potato shell, dividing it equally among all 6 skins. Top each with some pecans and bake for an additional 15 minutes. Serve piping hot.

Cookie-Cutter Vanilla Cookies

Cookie-Cutter Vanilla Frosting

Molasses Spice Cookies

Polenta Almond Cherry Cookies

Pistachio Joys

Coconut Pecan Chocolate Chunk Cookie Bars

Cranberry Walnut Shortbread

Hazelnut Buckwheat Shortbread
Dipped in Dark Chocolate

Christmas Fig and Spice Cake
with Creamy Citrus Frosting

Almond Bundt Cake

Pear Spice Cake

Braided "Challah" Bread

New Century Stollen Bread

Banana Walnut Bread

Holiday Cookies, Cakes, and Breads

I CAN'T HELP MYSELF—I think I enjoy developing cookie recipes more than any others. Cookies are such simple treasures and give so much pleasure to whip up, especially during the gray winters of Seattle, where I live. Having a nice long walk in the crisp, cold, and often damp air and then returning to a warm, bright kitchen to make cookies for my family is one of my greatest delights. There are cookie, cake, and bread recipes throughout this book, but I thought that Christmas and Hanukkah deserved their own special sweets section.

Cookie-Cutter Vanilla Cookies

Every holiday can be made even more fanciful with the addition of these treats, which can take on so many shapes and colors. I prefer to use natural food coloring, such as Nature's Flavors organic and gluten-free coloring, which works beautifully with the frosting recipe that follows this one. I like to shape these cookies into eggs for Easter, dreidels for Hanukkah, ornaments and trees for Christmas, four-leaf clovers for Saint Patrick's Day, and ghosts for Halloween. Roll up your sleeves and get ready to make a fun-filled mess with the kids!

MAKES ABOUT 24 COOKIES

> 2 tablespoons chia seeds
>
> 1½ cups water
>
> 3 cups brown rice flour, plus extra for rolling out dough and cutting cookies
>
> 1⅓ cups garbanzo bean flour
>
> 1 teaspoon baking powder
>
> ½ teaspoon baking soda
>
> ½ teaspoon sea salt
>
> 1 cup canola oil
>
> 1 cup Sucanat
>
> 1 teaspoon vanilla extract
>
> Cookie-Cutter Vanilla Frosting (page 47)

1. Preheat the oven to 350 degrees F. Generously dust your work surface with brown rice flour and place a plate with extra flour nearby. Lightly grease 2 cookie sheets.

2. Begin by soaking the chia seeds in the water for at least 15 minutes. In a medium bowl, whisk together the brown rice flour, garbanzo bean flour, baking powder, baking soda, and salt. In the bowl of a stand mixer fitted with the

paddle attachment, thoroughly combine the canola oil, Sucanat, and vanilla on low speed. Add the dry ingredients, alternating with the chia seeds and their soaking liquid, until the dough has attained a smooth consistency.

3. Now comes the really fun part. On your floured work surface, gently knead the cookie dough a few times and then roll it out, adding flour as needed to keep the dough from sticking, until it is about ¼ inch thick. Using your favorite seasonal cookie cutters, cut out shapes, dipping your cutter in a little rice flour between each cookie. With a floured spatula, transfer cookies to the baking sheets and bake for 15 minutes, or until the cookies are lightly browned. Let the cookies cool on the baking sheet before frosting.

Cookie-Cutter Vanilla Frosting

Reminiscent of buttercream, this creamy vanilla frosting is very easy to work with. Someone in the kitchen will be sure to lick the bowl clean!

MAKES ENOUGH TO FROST 24 COOKIES

> 1½ cups powdered evaporated cane juice
>
> ½ cup coconut oil
>
> ⅛ teaspoon sea salt
>
> 1½ teaspoons vanilla extract
>
> 1 tablespoon boiling water
>
> 2 tablespoons maple syrup
>
> Organic, gluten-free liquid food coloring (optional)

1. Sift the powdered evaporated cane juice into a large bowl; add the coconut oil. Using an electric mixer on low speed, beat until the mixture is soft and the sugar is incorporated. Add the salt and vanilla and mix briefly. Slowly add the boiling water and maple syrup as you whip the frosting. Continue to mix, pausing every so often to scrape down the sides of the bowl with a spatula.

2. When the frosting has attained a smooth, fluffy consistency, add the food coloring a few drops at a time until the color is to your liking. The frosting can be stored in an airtight container in the cupboard for up to four days. If it has been stored for a few days, heat gently in a double boiler and rewhip it prior to using.

Molasses Spice Cookies

Crisp on the outside, chewy on the inside, and full of spicy surprise—these dark, flavorful cookies are made sophisticated by the subtle addition of coriander. Dusting them with powdered sugar gives them a festive look, but they are also delicious by themselves.

MAKES ABOUT 24 COOKIES

½ cup extra-virgin olive oil

½ cup molasses

½ cup Sucanat

2 teaspoons vanilla extract

1 teaspoon sea salt

1 teaspoon ground ginger

¼ teaspoon ground coriander

½ teaspoon ground cloves

2 cups brown rice flour

1 cup buckwheat flour

1 teaspoon baking powder

½ cup water

1 cup dried currants

Powdered evaporated cane juice, for dusting

1. Preheat the oven to 350 degrees F and lightly grease 2 baking sheets.

2. In the bowl of a stand mixer fitted with the paddle attachment, or in a large bowl and using an electric mixer, add the olive oil, molasses, Sucanat, vanilla,

salt, ginger, coriander, and cloves. Mix on low speed until well combined. Add the brown rice and buckwheat flours and baking powder. Add the water and mix to form a smooth dough. Add the currants and mix on low speed to incorporate.

3. Use your hands to form the dough into 2-inch balls, transferring them to the baking sheets as you work. Gently press down with your palm to slightly flatten the balls. Bake for 15 minutes, or until puffed and set. Cool on baking sheets, then lightly dust cookies with powdered evaporated cane juice.

Polenta Almond Cherry Cookies

These may be my all-time favorite cookies. A bold statement indeed! For a cookie sans chocolate (one of my most beloved dessert additions), these are unbeatable. The brightness of the yellow polenta against the cherry-red center adds cheer to any winter day.

MAKES ABOUT 24 COOKIES

½ cup coconut oil

¼ cup maple syrup

1 teaspoon vanilla extract

½ teaspoon sea salt

1 cup almond meal

½ cup quick-cooking polenta

½ cup brown rice flour

One 15-ounce can bing cherries

1. Preheat the oven to 350 degrees F.

2. In a large mixing bowl combine the coconut oil, maple syrup, vanilla, and salt. Add the almond meal, polenta, and brown rice flour, mixing well. Drop tablespoon-size portions of dough onto ungreased baking sheets, spaced 2 inches apart, as the cookies will spread while baking. Place a cherry in the center of each cookie. Bake for 20 minutes, or until lightly browned.

Pistachio Joys

These pretty Pistachio Joys have a snowy winter look. If you like to give away tins of cookies around the holidays, this is an excellent one to include. They are "buttery" and tender but hold up well.

MAKES ABOUT 24 MINIATURE COOKIES

½ cup coconut oil

¼ cup maple syrup

1 teaspoon vanilla extract

1⅔ cups brown rice flour

⅛ teaspoon sea salt

½ cup shelled pistachios, finely chopped, plus 24 extra for decorating cookies (optional)

Powdered evaporated cane juice, for dusting (optional)

1. Preheat the oven to 350 degrees F.

2. In the bowl of a stand mixer fitted with the paddle attachment, or in a large bowl and using a hand mixer, cream together the coconut oil, maple syrup, and vanilla. Add the flour, salt, and chopped pistachios. Mix well until a smooth dough forms. Pull off pieces of the dough and roll between your palms into 1½-inch balls, transferring them to 2 ungreased cookie sheets as you work. Lightly press a whole pistachio in the center of each cookie. Bake for 15 minutes, or until lightly browned, then cool on the pans. For a festive look, dust the cookies while they're hot with powdered evaporated cane juice.

Coconut Pecan Chocolate Chunk Cookie Bars

These bars meet all my criteria for a truly satisfying cookie experience: they are slightly crisp yet have soft gooey bits; the pecans offer crunch; the coconut lends texture; the chocolate is abundant; and the subtle tahini adds body. Plus, cut into striking triangles, they have a very artistic appearance.

MAKES 12 TO 16 BARS

½ cup coconut oil

¼ cup maple syrup

1 teaspoon vanilla extract

½ teaspoon sea salt

1 cup coconut flour

1 cup unsweetened shredded coconut

¼ cup water

½ cup finely chopped pecans

5½ ounces dark chocolate (72% cacao), finely chopped

½ cup tahini

1. Preheat the oven to 350 degrees F.

2. In a large mixing bowl, thoroughly combine the coconut oil, maple syrup, vanilla, and salt. Add the coconut flour, coconut, and water, and mix until a smooth dough forms. Add the pecans, chocolate, and tahini, mixing well. Press the cookie dough into a round 10-inch springform pan. Bake for 17 minutes, or until lightly browned. Cool in the pan and slice into wedges. Serve on a platter, attractively arranged.

Cranberry Walnut Shortbread

This shortbread is oh-so-very tasty and sophisticated, yet simple. Be sure to finely chop the walnuts for an even texture.

MAKES 10 SHORTBREAD TRIANGLES

½ cup coconut oil

¼ cup maple syrup

1 teaspoon vanilla extract

1 cup buckwheat flour

½ teaspoon sea salt

½ teaspoon ground cinnamon

1 cup finely chopped walnuts

½ cup dried cranberries

1. Preheat the oven to 350 degrees F and lightly grease a 9-inch tart pan.

2. In the bowl of a stand mixer fitted with the paddle attachment, combine the coconut oil, maple syrup, and vanilla. Add the buckwheat flour, salt, and cinnamon; mix until the dough is smooth. Add the walnuts and cranberries and mix on low speed to incorporate. Press the dough into the tart pan and bake for 20 minutes, or until darkened around the edges. Slice into 10 triangles while still warm and then let cool completely.

Hazelnut Buckwheat Shortbread Dipped in Dark Chocolate

These shortbread cookies will knock Santa's socks off! My husband thinks they'd knock Hanukkah Harry's socks off, too.

MAKES ABOUT 12 COOKIES

½ cup coconut oil

¼ cup date sugar

⅛ teaspoon sea salt, plus a pinch

⅛ teaspoon ground cardamom

⅛ teaspoon ground cloves

1 teaspoon vanilla extract

1 cup buckwheat flour, plus extra for rolling out cookies

½ cup hazelnut flour

¼ cup water

3 ounces dark chocolate (70% cacao)

2 tablespoons coconut oil

1. Preheat the oven to 350 degrees F and generously dust your work surface with buckwheat flour. Lightly grease a cookie sheet and set aside.

2. In a large mixing bowl, using a wooden spoon or an electric mixer, cream the coconut oil and date sugar. Add the ⅛ teaspoon salt, cardamom, cloves, and vanilla. Mix in the buckwheat and hazelnut flours, and water. When the dough is thoroughly combined, turn it out onto your work surface. Liberally dust the rolling pin with buckwheat flour, and roll the dough out to about ⅛ inch thick.

Using your favorite cookie cutter, cut out shapes (I like to use a glass dipped in flour as my cookie cutter). With a floured spatula, transfer cookies to the cookie sheet and bake for 20 minutes. Remove from the oven; leave the cookies on the pan to cool.

3. Meanwhile, in a double boiler or using a metal bowl placed on top of a pot of simmering water, melt the chocolate, coconut oil, and a pinch of salt. Whisk thoroughly and remove from the heat. You may dip your cookies in the chocolate, or using a spoon, cover half of each cookie with a spoonful of chocolate. Alternatively, you can drizzle chocolate on the cookies for a lacy look. (You may have leftover chocolate.) Let sit for 1 hour at room temperature before serving.

Christmas Fig and Spice Cake with Creamy Citrus Frosting

This cake is dark, moist, and rich, with morsels of figs and background flavors of seasonal spices, topped with frosting as white as fresh snow.

MAKES ONE 9-INCH CAKE

FOR THE CAKE:

½ cup extra-virgin olive oil

1 cup maple syrup

1 cup water

2 teaspoons vanilla extract

1½ cups buckwheat flour

1 cup hazelnut flour

1½ teaspoons baking soda

½ teaspoon sea salt

1 teaspoon ground cinnamon

½ teaspoon ground cloves

Zest of 2 medium oranges (about 5 tablespoons)

1 cup dried figs, sliced very thinly

FOR THE FROSTING:

1 cup coconut oil

2 cups powdered evaporated cane juice

¼ teaspoon sea salt

2 teaspoons vanilla extract

Zest of 2 medium oranges (about 5 tablespoons)

1. To make the cake, preheat the oven to 350 degrees F and lightly grease a 9-inch cake pan.

2. In a large mixing bowl, combine the olive oil, maple syrup, water, and vanilla. In a separate bowl, combine the buckwheat and hazelnut flours, baking soda, salt, cinnamon, and cloves. Using an electric mixer, beat at low speed until the ingredients are combined. Mix the dry ingredients into the wet ingredients and thoroughly combine. Fold in the orange zest and figs. Pour the batter into the cake pan and bake for 50 minutes. It's done when the cake bounces back after gently pressing a finger into the top.

3. To make the frosting, combine all the ingredients in a large mixing bowl. Using an electric mixer, beat at low speed until combined. Increase speed to high and whip until the frosting is creamy and smooth. You may need to scrape down the sides of the bowl a few times to be sure all the ingredients have been incorporated.

4. When the cake has completely cooled, frost it using a cake spatula or butter knife. For an extra-rich treat, carefully split the cake in half using a serrated knife and frost in the middle as well.

Almond Bundt Cake

I love the sculptural quality of a good old-fashioned Bundt cake. The sweet almond flavor of this cake, combined with its heavenly, moist texture, makes for an ideal sweet course.

MAKES ONE BUNDT CAKE

> 1 cup almond meal
>
> 2 cups brown rice flour
>
> ½ teaspoon sea salt
>
> 2 teaspoons baking soda
>
> ⅔ cup extra-virgin olive oil or canola oil
>
> 1½ cups water
>
> 2 teaspoons vanilla extract
>
> 1½ cups maple syrup

1. Preheat the oven to 350 degrees F and grease a standard-size Bundt pan.

2. In a large mixing bowl, combine the almond meal, brown rice flour, salt, and baking soda. In another mixing bowl, combine the olive oil, water, vanilla, and maple syrup. Add the wet ingredients to the dry ingredients and mix thoroughly. Pour the batter into the Bundt pan. Bake for 1 hour, or until a toothpick inserted in the center comes out clean. Let cool completely before removing the cake from the pan.

Pear Spice Cake

Winter pears with fragrant spices baking together in your oven on a chilly day—what could be lovelier? Perhaps sharing a slice with friends accompanied by a pot of hot tea. This cake is really perfect for any time of day. It is mildly sweet and works equally well for breakfast or dessert.

MAKES ONE 10-INCH CAKE

½ cup extra-virgin olive oil

1 cup water

½ cup maple syrup

½ cup date sugar

1 teaspoon vanilla extract

2¼ cups teff flour

1 teaspoon baking soda

¾ teaspoon sea salt

1 teaspoon ground cinnamon

½ teaspoon ground cloves

1 large pear, cored and very thinly sliced

1 tablespoon dark brown sugar

1. Preheat the oven to 350 degrees F and grease a 10-inch springform pan.

2. In a large mixing bowl, combine the olive oil, water, maple syrup, date sugar, and vanilla. In a separate bowl, combine the teff flour, baking soda, salt, cinnamon, and cloves. Gradually incorporate the dry ingredients into the wet ingredients and combine well. Pour the batter into the pan and arrange the pears in overlapping concentric circles covering the entire cake. Sprinkle the pears with the brown sugar. Bake for 45 minutes, or until the cake bounces back after gently pressing a finger into the top. Let cool slightly before serving.

Braided "Challah" Bread

My goal for this recipe was to create a gluten-free, vegan challah with unrefined flours. Traditional challah is made with eggs, which really add to its light, soft texture. My version is indeed heavier and denser, but delicious just the same. And the pieces of dough braided together still represent arms intertwined as a symbol of love.

MAKES ONE LOAF

¼ cup extra-virgin olive oil

1 tablespoon honey or agave syrup

¾ cup lukewarm water

1 tablespoon active dry yeast

2½ cups teff flour, plus extra for dusting the loaf

1 cup brown rice flour, plus extra for kneading the dough

¼ cup mashed cooked yam

1 teaspoon sea salt

1 teaspoon xanthan gum

1. Preheat the oven to 350 degrees F. Generously dust your work surface with brown rice flour.

2. In a large mixing bowl, combine the olive oil, honey, water, and yeast. In a separate bowl, combine the teff and brown rice flours, yam, salt, and xanthan gum.

3. As soon as the yeast is active (it will take 3 to 5 minutes), gradually incorporate the dry ingredients into the wet ingredients. This can be done by hand or with an electric mixer on low speed. Be sure not to overmix. As soon as the dough forms, remove it from the bowl and gently knead it for 3 or 4 turns on your

floured work surface. Divide the dough into 3 equal parts. Roll each piece of dough into a 10-inch-long rope. Transfer to a floured baking sheet and braid the dough ropes together, being careful to keep them snug but not to tight, as they will expand a bit while baking. Tuck the top and bottom ends of the braid under. Dust the loaf with teff flour. Bake for about 1 hour and 10 minutes, or until golden and firm to the touch.

New Century Stollen Bread

This traditional bread originated in Germany more than five hundred years ago. It began more as a bread than a cake, but over the years it has evolved to become sweeter and sweeter, containing candied fruits and often covered with a glaze. My creation is somewhere in between the more cake-like modern stollen and the original bread.

MAKES ONE LOAF

¼ cup extra-virgin olive oil

1½ tablespoons honey or agave syrup

¾ cup lukewarm water

1 tablespoon active dry yeast

2½ cups teff flour

1 cup brown rice flour, plus extra for kneading the dough

1 teaspoon sea salt

1 teaspoon xanthan gum

¼ cup mashed cooked yam

½ cup dried cranberries

½ cup dried currants

¼ cup candied orange peel

½ cup chopped blanched almonds

Zest of one medium lemon (about 2 teaspoons)

Powdered evaporated cane juice, for dusting loaf

1. Preheat the oven to 350 degrees F and generously dust your work surface with brown rice flour.

2. In a large mixing bowl, combine the olive oil, honey, water, and yeast. In a separate bowl, combine the teff and brown rice flours, salt, xanthan gum, yam, cranberries, currants, orange peel, almonds, and lemon zest.

3. As soon as the yeast is active (it will take 3 to 5 minutes), gradually incorporate the dry ingredients into the wet ingredients. This can be done by hand or with an electric mixer on low speed. Be sure not to overmix. As soon as the dough forms, remove it from the bowl and gently knead it for 3 or 4 turns on your floured work surface. Shape it into a 10-inch-long *bâtarde*. Transfer the loaf to a baking sheet, and bake for about 1 hour and 10 minutes, or until golden and firm to the touch. When the bread is cool, dust it liberally with sifted powdered evaporated cane juice.

Stuffed Artichokes Amore

Artichokes strike me as a romantic vegetable. Perhaps it is because I imagine they are often shared over candlelit tables in Italian restaurants, or maybe it is due to the sensuality of their shape. Regardless, I believe this tantalizing recipe will contribute to an amorous Valentine's Day.

4 medium artichokes

1 medium lemon

3 slices of your favorite gluten-free bread

¼ cup walnuts, almonds, or pine nuts

2 tablespoons extra-virgin olive oil

4 cloves garlic

1 teaspoon dried thyme leaves

½ teaspoon dried oregano

½ teaspoon dried rosemary

½ teaspoon sea salt

Freshly ground pepper

1. Preheat the oven to 350 degrees F.

2. Begin by cutting off the bottom stem and top quarter of each artichoke. With a spoon, scoop the leaves from the middle until you can see the artichoke heart. Continue to scrape until the inside cavity is free of the "hairs" of the thistle and surrounding prickly leaves. Squeeze a little lemon juice into each prepared artichoke.

3. To make the stuffing, toast the bread and then slice it into small pieces. Put the bread pieces, walnuts, olive oil, garlic, thyme, oregano, rosemary, and salt into a

food processor and briefly pulse until the bread has formed coarse crumbs and the mixture is combined. Season with pepper to taste.

4. Place the artichokes in a shallow baking dish and evenly divide the stuffing among their centers and some outer pockets between the leaves. Fill the pan with about 1½ inches of hot water and steam in the oven for 30 minutes, checking them at 20 minutes. Depending on the size of your artichokes, they may take more or less time—they will be slightly darker green in color when they're done. Check by tasting an artichoke leaf to see if its flesh comes off easily. Be sure not to overbake.

Porcini Mushroom Risotto

Risotto has been made for centuries, so it didn't take much creative prowess for me to bring this recipe to life. I simply compiled my own combination of flavors while working with an ancient technique. The deep, rich flavor of the porcini mushrooms is absorbed by the arborio rice, resulting in what feels like a succulent indulgence.

2 ounces (about 1 cup) dried porcini mushrooms

4 cups boiling water

2 medium onions, finely chopped

3 cloves garlic, minced

¼ cup extra-virgin olive oil

1¾ cups arborio rice, rinsed to remove excess starch

1½ cups white wine

Pinch of sea salt

Freshly ground pepper

½ cup finely chopped Italian parsley, for garnish

1. Soak the dried porcini mushrooms in the boiling water for 1 hour. Gently lift the mushrooms out of the water, being careful not to stir up any grit that may have settled at the bottom of the dish. Squeeze the mushrooms dry, then coarsely chop them. Strain the mushroom soaking liquid through a fine-mesh sieve lined with cheesecloth or a paper towel. In a small saucepan, bring the liquid, which is your mushroom stock, to a simmer, maintaining that simmer throughout the risotto-making process.

2. In a large soup pot over medium-low heat, sauté the onions and garlic in the olive oil for 10 minutes. Add the mushrooms and cook for another 2 minutes. Then add the rice and cook, stirring, until it becomes slightly translucent,

about 7 minutes. Increase the heat to medium-high and add the wine and salt. Cook, stirring continuously, until the wine is almost completely absorbed, about 15 minutes. Add a ladleful of mushroom stock, again cooking until it is all absorbed, stirring all the while. Continue this process until all the mushroom stock is absorbed into the rice. Taste a piece of rice; it should be tender yet firm to the bite. Cover the risotto, remove it from the heat, and let it sit for 3 minutes before serving. Season to taste with pepper and additional salt. Garnish with the parsley.

Simplest Steamed Greens

This dish is indeed very simple, but it is one of my personal favorites. It is the perfect accompaniment to almost any meal. These dark greens balance the more complex flavors of the other dishes on this menu.

1 bunch Swiss chard, washed well, stems and center ribs cut out and chopped into small pieces, leaves coarsely chopped and kept separate

1 bunch purple kale, washed well, stems and inner ribs discarded, leaves coarsely chopped

¼ cup extra-virgin olive oil

Juice of ½ medium lemon (about 1½ tablespoons)

½ teaspoon sea salt

1. In a large pot fitted with a steamer insert, bring 2 cups water to a boil. Place the chard stems and ribs on the bottom of the steamer, followed by the kale leaves, with the chard leaves on top. Steam the greens for about 5 minutes, or until they are tender. Place the greens in a serving bowl with the olive oil, lemon juice, and salt, and toss well.

Miniature Chocolate Hazelnut Cakes

The combination of chocolate and hazelnuts can be traced back as far as the early 1600s to a Spanish recipe. What a remarkably pleasing discovery to combine these two special ingredients! These cakes are very moist and decadent.

MAKES 1 DOZEN 2¾-INCH CUPCAKES OR SIX 5-INCH CAKES

FOR THE CAKES:

> ¾ cup brown rice flour
>
> ½ cup hazelnut flour
>
> ½ cup unsweetened cocoa powder
>
> ½ cup packed dark brown sugar
>
> 1½ teaspoons baking soda
>
> ¾ teaspoon sea salt
>
> ½ cup canola or extra-virgin olive oil
>
> ½ cup maple syrup
>
> 1 teaspoon vanilla extract
>
> 1 cup water

FOR THE FROSTING:

> 5½ ounces dark chocolate (70% cacao), chopped
>
> 1 cup coconut oil
>
> 1 teaspoon vanilla extract
>
> ¼ teaspoon sea salt
>
> ¼ teaspoon ground cinnamon

1. To make the cakes, first preheat the oven to 350 degrees F.

2. In a large bowl, combine the brown rice and hazelnut flours, cocoa powder, brown sugar, baking soda, and salt. In a separate bowl, combine the oil, maple syrup, vanilla, and water. Whisk the wet ingredients into the dry ingredients. Pour into 12 paper-lined 2¾-inch cupcake tins or 6 ungreased 5-inch rame- kins. For cupcakes, bake for 30 minutes. For larger cakes, bake for 45 minutes, or until the cake bounces back after gently pressing a finger into the top. Let cool while you make the frosting.

3. To make the frosting, in a double boiler or using a metal bowl placed on top of a pot of simmering water, melt the chocolate. When the chocolate is com- pletely melted, transfer it to the bowl of a stand mixer fitted with the paddle attachment. Add the coconut oil, vanilla, salt, and cinnamon, and beat on medium speed to combine. Place the mixing bowl in the refrigerator for 30 minutes to chill the frosting. When cool, scrape down the sides of the bowl and beat again on high speed until light and fluffy, 2 to 3 minutes. Frost cooled cakes and devour!

MENU

....

Portobello and Shiitake Mushroom Stew

Rosemary Roasted Carrots and New Potatoes

Red and Green Caraway Cabbage

Irish Soda Bread

Late Winter Apple Tarte

Cookie-Cutter Vanilla Cookies (page 44),
in the shape of shamrocks

....

SERVES 6 TO 8

Saint Patrick's Day

SAINT PATRICK'S DAY HAS BECOME such a jolly holiday, full of magic, merriment, feasting, and celebrating. There's something about the music and charm of the Irish that reaches into the heart and stirs up laughter, love, loss, and love again. On my daughter's first birthday, our dear friend and neighbor Kathy invited us to join her at a café near our home where she would be making music with her Celtic band. Joseph, Lilli, and I arrived late to a full house of folks dressed in green, rejoicing in the gorgeous sounds of yore. Somehow Kathy spotted us in the back and announced to the audience that Lilli had just arrived and that she was one year old that very day. The crowd, in a state of deep emotion from all the drinking and songs of life and death, burst into the most beautiful and heartfelt happy birthday song I've ever heard. It was a moment I will never forget.

Except for the shamrock cookies, everything on this menu is really best made that day. The soda bread is outstanding, and no doubt you will be making it frequently throughout the year.

There are so many truly witty and wise Irish proverbs, but I would like to leave you with this rather undeniable and clever one: *Chan fhiach curium gun a comhradh*—a feast is no use without good conversation. Enjoy your company and eat well!

Portobello and Shiitake Mushroom Stew

I created this very hearty stew to enjoy with a stout beer on Saint Patrick's Day. The mushrooms take on a meaty texture and rich flavor. My father's side of the family are proud Irish folk, and I hope this recipe is reminiscent of the roasts and stews enjoyed during long-ago family gatherings.

2 ounces (about 1 cup) dried shiitake mushrooms

4 cups boiling water

1 medium onion, diced

2 tablespoons extra-virgin olive oil

4 medium portobello mushrooms (1¼ to 1½ pounds total), thinly sliced

½ cup red wine

¼ cup tamari

1 tablespoon balsamic vinegar

1 sprig fresh rosemary, finely chopped

1 tablespoon chopped fresh thyme, plus 8 additional sprigs for garnish

1¼ pounds new red potatoes (about 15 small), chopped into bite-size chunks

One 14.5-ounce can diced tomatoes

1. Reconstitute the dried shiitake mushrooms in the boiling water for about 20 minutes. Strain the mushrooms, reserving the soaking liquid. Trim away and discard the tough stems. Thinly slice the mushroom tops.

2. Meanwhile, in a large pot, sauté the onion in the olive oil over low heat until the onion is transparent, about 10 minutes. Add the sliced shiitake and portobello mushrooms. Increase the heat to medium-high and add the wine, tamari,

and balsamic vinegar. Cook until the mushrooms release their juices and absorb the added liquid, about 10 minutes. Add the reserved shiitake soaking liquid, rosemary, thyme, and potatoes. Increase heat to high; when the stew boils, reduce the heat to low. Add the diced tomatoes, cover, and simmer for about 1 hour. Garnish with thyme sprigs.

Rosemary Roasted Carrots and New Potatoes

On a chilly spring day such as Saint Patrick's, this dish is sure to satisfy. Crispy on the outside and tender on the inside, the potatoes, intermingled with fresh rosemary and the sweetness of roasted carrots, are oh so enjoyable.

1 pound new red potatoes (about 10 small), halved

½ pound carrots, peeled and cut diagonally into ½-inch pieces

¼ cup canola oil

3 tablespoons minced fresh rosemary

4 cloves garlic, minced

1 teaspoon sea salt

½ teaspoon freshly ground pepper

1. Preheat the oven to 400 degrees F.

2. Combine all the ingredients in a large bowl and toss well to coat the potatoes and carrots with the seasonings and oil. Pour the contents of the bowl onto a large baking sheet and roast the vegetables for about 50 minutes, or until the exteriors are crisp and the interiors can be easily pierced with a fork. (Halfway through cooking, using tongs or a spatula, turn the potatoes and carrots so that they brown evenly.) Transfer to a serving bowl and season to taste with additional salt and pepper.

Red and Green Caraway Cabbage

In Ireland, where the climate is cool, cabbage is a dependable crop and has been enjoyed alongside potatoes for a very long time. It is one of my favorite vegetables, and it requires very little preparation.

1 small red cabbage, cored and finely chopped

1 large green cabbage, cored and finely chopped

2 teaspoons toasted caraway seeds

⅓ cup extra-virgin olive oil

1 teaspoon sea salt

Freshly ground pepper

1. In a large pot fitted with a steamer insert, bring 2 cups water to a boil. Place the cabbage in the steamer and steam for about 10 minutes, or until the cabbage is tender. Depending on the size of your steamer, you may need to do this in two batches. If so, toss the first batch of cabbage with half of the olive oil and keep it warm in a covered bowl in your oven. Toss all of the cooked cabbage with the caraway seeds, remaining olive oil, and salt, and season to taste with pepper.

Irish Soda Bread

Growing up, this was a bread I looked forward to every Saint Patrick's Day. Irish soda bread was a staple in my grandmother's house, and after we moved to the West Coast, my mother would continue the tradition every spring. Here is my gluten-free and vegan version.

MAKES I LOAF

> 3 cups teff flour, plus extra for kneading the dough
>
> 1 teaspoon xanthan gum
>
> 1 teaspoon baking soda
>
> ½ teaspoon sea salt
>
> ½ cup dark raisins
>
> ½ teaspoon caraway seeds
>
> 2 teaspoons date sugar
>
> 2 tablespoons extra-virgin olive oil
>
> 1 cup water

1. Preheat the oven to 350 degrees F. Generously dust your work surface with teff flour.

2. In a large mixing bowl or the bowl of a stand mixer fitted with the paddle attachment, combine the teff flour, xanthan gum, baking soda, salt, raisins, caraway seeds, and date sugar. Add the oil and water and mix well until a smooth dough forms. On the floured work surface, gently knead dough with just a few turns and shape into a round 6-inch loaf. Score the loaf with a crisscross and bake for 50 minutes, or until browned and firm to the touch.

Late Winter Apple Tarte

This delicious dessert is somewhere between a pie and a cake. The bottom crust is slightly prebaked and will appear rather soft, which may seem unusual. Do continue with the recipe even though the crust will seem somewhat underdone—your finished masterpiece will be exceptional.

FOR THE CRUST:

> 1¼ cups almond meal
>
> 1 cup teff flour
>
> ⅔ cup coconut oil
>
> ¼ teaspoon sea salt
>
> ½ teaspoon ground cinnamon

FOR THE FILLING:

> 2 medium apples, peeled, cored, and very thinly sliced
>
> ½ cup canned unsweetened coconut milk
>
> ½ teaspoon ground cinnamon

1. Preheat the oven to 350 degrees F.

2. To make the tart crust, in the bowl of a stand mixer fitted with a dough hook, combine 1 cup of the almond meal, the teff flour, coconut oil, salt, and cinnamon. Mix on low speed until a soft, pielike dough forms. Reserve ¼ cup of dough for the top of the tart and press the rest of the dough into a 9-inch tart pan. Bake for 15 minutes, or until barely golden.

3. While the bottom crust is baking, prepare the filling. In a medium bowl, combine the apples, coconut milk, and cinnamon. Spread the filling evenly in the prebaked tart crust, arranging the apples in concentric circles. Sprinkle with bits of the reserved tart dough and the remaining ¼ cup almond meal. Bake for an additional 45 minutes, or until golden.

MENU

....

Charoset

Miniature Buckwheat Pancakes
with Dill Cashew Cream Sauce

Matzo Ball Vegetable Soup

Mint and Basil Citrus Salad

Stuffed Cabbage Rolls with Chardonnay Sauce

Carrot Tzimmes

Fresh Fruit Tart

....

SERVES 4 GENEROUSLY

Passover

When I designed this Passover menu, I gathered stories from my husband Joseph about his family's Passover dinners. I also researched what has traditionally been served over the years. However, I'm not sure that these two sources completely mesh: for example, Joseph told me that part of his family's tradition was a contest between him and his brother over who could eat the biggest bite of horseradish!

What really fascinates me about this particular holiday meal is that certain ingredients, such as horseradish, serve as specific reminders of Jewish history, emphasizing the important role that food has long played in our lives.

This menu is rather elaborate, so making some dishes in advance will be helpful. The fresh fruit tart is sensational—I make the crust and filling the day before and assemble the tart the day it is to be served. The matzo ball soup with fresh herbs is a must, but some advance preparation will make all the difference in pulling the dish together gracefully: I recommend making a homemade vegetable broth the day before or having vegetable bouillon handy. The matzo bread and matzo balls can also be made the day before and stored in an airtight container in the refrigerator. Before serving, just heat up the broth and drop slightly warmed matzo balls into each bowl. Lastly, the cashew cream that tops the miniature buckwheat pancakes can also be made one day ahead. The rest of the menu will be tastiest when made the evening it is to be enjoyed. *L' Chaim*—to life!

Charoset

This is such a delicious dish and so easy to prepare. I find myself eating the leftovers as a dessert! Charoset reminds me somewhat of a chutney, with the addition of nuts and wine. To create this one, I combined my favorite ingredients from a number of recipes. I didn't grow up participating in the Passover tradition, so I was fascinated to learn that mashing the ingredients together with a mortar and pestle serves as a reminder of how clay bricks were once made during a time of oppression. The sweetness of the dish is meant to celebrate freedom in this present time.

> 1 cup finely chopped toasted walnuts
>
> 2 medium apples, peeled, cored, and finely chopped
>
> 1 cup finely chopped pitted prunes
>
> ½ cup red wine
>
> 2 tablespoons maple syrup
>
> 1 teaspoon ground cinnamon

1. Combine all the ingredients in a large pestle, mashing them with the mortar. (Alternatively, pulse briefly in a food processor until a chunky consistency is achieved.) Pour the charoset into a beautiful serving bowl and cover until ready to serve. This dish is meant to be enjoyed at room temperature.

Miniature Buckwheat Pancakes with Dill Cashew Cream Sauce

You will certainly impress yourself and your guests with this fancy appetizer. To save time, the pancake batter can be made a few hours in advance, and the cashew cream can be made the day before serving.

FOR THE CASHEW CREAM:

    1½ cups raw cashews, soaked in water for 8 hours, then drained

    Juice of 2 medium lemons (about 6 tablespoons)

    3 tablespoons capers

    2 tablespoons chopped fresh dill

    ¼ cup water

    Sea salt and freshly ground pepper

FOR THE PANCAKES:

    ½ cup buckwheat flour

    1 cup teff flour

    1 tablespoon extra-virgin olive oil

    ½ teaspoon sea salt

    ½ teaspoon poppy seeds

    ½ teaspoon ground coriander

    1 cup water

    24 small fresh dill sprigs, for garnish

1. To make the cashew cream, combine the cashews, lemon juice, 1 tablespoon of the capers, dill, and ¼ cup water in a blender and purée until the cream is smooth. Season to taste with salt and pepper. Transfer the sauce to a bowl and fold in the remaining 2 tablespoons of capers. Set aside or chill overnight in the refrigerator. Bring to room temperature before serving.

2. To make the pancakes, whisk all the ingredients together in a large mixing bowl. In a greased skillet (I like to use a cast-iron skillet lightly greased with coconut oil) over medium heat, drop tablespoon-size portions of batter and fry pancakes for 3 minutes per side, or until slightly firm. Keep cooked pancakes warm in the oven while you fry the remaining batter. To serve, place a dollop of the cashew cream on top of each pancake and garnish with a sprig of dill.

Matzo Ball Vegetable Soup

My husband says these matzo balls are remarkably like the ones he remembers while growing up. I've spruced them up by adding a generous amount of fresh herbs.

Gluten-Free Matzo Bread (recipe follows)

1 medium Yukon gold potato, peeled, boiled, and chopped, ¼ cup potato cooking liquid reserved

¼ cup finely chopped fresh basil

¼ cup finely chopped fresh oregano

¼ cup finely chopped fresh Italian parsley

¼ cup extra-virgin olive oil

½ teaspoon sea salt

Freshly ground pepper

8 cups vegetable broth

1. Make the Gluten-Free Matzo Bread, following directions for making matzo balls for soup. Allow the bread to cool.

2. To make the matzo balls, break the matzo bread into pieces and place in a food processor. Pulse until little pearls of bread crumbs form. For this recipe, the matzo bread is somewhat softer than usual, so expect the pearls to be a touch doughy. Add the potato, basil, oregano, parsley, olive oil, salt, and reserved potato cooking liquid. Season to taste with pepper. Pulse until the dough holds together. Roll the dough between your palms to form 2-inch ovals; when you are finished, you should have 16 matzo balls. Set aside.

3. In a soup pot over medium-high heat, heat the vegetable stock until it is piping hot. Ladle the stock into 4 bowls and place 4 matzo balls in each bowl.

Gluten-Free Matzo Bread

I devised this recipe to create the matzo meal I use for matzo balls in the Matzo Ball Vegetable Soup. I love the way the matzo balls taste with this bread alternative serving as a wonderful base.

> 1 cup brown rice flour
> ½ cup coconut flour
> 1½ cups water

1. Preheat the oven to 350 degrees F and lightly grease a baking sheet.

2. In the bowl of a stand mixer fitted with the paddle attachment or in a large mixing bowl, combine all the ingredients and mix until a smooth dough forms. Press the dough out onto the baking sheet, forming a 10-inch circle; it should be about ¼ inch thick. Using a fork, prick the dough with holes all over. If using the bread to create matzo balls for soup, bake for 30 minutes, or until golden. For matzo bread to be served as is, bake for an additional 20 minutes (50 minutes total), or until firm. Allow the bread to cool before serving.

Mint and Basil Citrus Salad

The combination of mint and basil with citrus is so refreshing and zesty. I always appreciate a fresh salad with my meals, and this vividly colored salad complements the other dishes on the Passover menu beautifully.

2 large oranges

1 large grapefruit

1 fennel bulb, shaved or very thinly sliced

¼ cup fresh mint, sliced into thin ribbons

¼ cup fresh basil, sliced into thin ribbons

Juice of ½ medium lemon (about 1½ tablespoons)

⅓ cup extra-virgin olive oil

Sea salt and freshly ground pepper

½ cup toasted pine nuts

1. Cut off the tops and bottoms of the oranges and grapefruit; using a sharp knife, remove the peel and all of the white pith from each fruit. Hold the fruits over a medium bowl (to catch any juices that may release in the process) and separate the citrus segments. Place the citrus in a large bowl, reserving the released juice. Add the fennel, mint, and basil.

2. In a small separate bowl, combine the reserved juices, lemon juice, and olive oil, and season to taste with salt and pepper. Whisk the dressing well and toss with the salad. Before serving, top with the pine nuts.

Stuffed Cabbage Rolls with Chardonnay Sauce

Holishkes *is the Yiddish word for a dish of stuffed cabbage rolls. It is usually served during the Jewish festival of Sukkot in the fall but can be enjoyed anytime. Traditionally the* holishkes *are stuffed with meat. The filling in these rolls is of course not meat, but the dish is nonetheless very hearty, satisfying, and rich.*

FOR THE ROLLS:

> 3 shallots, quartered
>
> 2 cloves garlic, smashed
>
> 3 tablespoons extra-virgin olive oil
>
> 12 ounces chanterelle mushrooms, roughly chopped
>
> ½ cup chardonnay
>
> ¼ cup fresh thyme leaves, finely chopped
>
> ¾ cup slivered almonds
>
> ½ cup pecans
>
> 12 large napa cabbage leaves

FOR THE SAUCE:

> 1 medium onion, finely chopped
>
> 2 tablespoons extra-virgin olive oil
>
> 1½ cups chardonnay
>
> 1 cup vegetable stock
>
> 12 ounces tomato paste
>
> 1 tablespoon evaporated cane juice
>
> 1 tablespoon herbes de Provence
>
> ½ teaspoon sea salt
>
> Freshly ground pepper

1. To make the cabbage rolls, in a large skillet over low heat, sauté the shallots and garlic in the olive oil until the shallots have softened and are just beginning to turn golden, about 10 minutes. Add the mushrooms and cook until they begin to release their juices and brown slightly, about 10 minutes. Increase the heat, add the chardonnay and thyme, and bring to a boil. Cook until almost all the wine has evaporated, about 15 minutes. Let the mushroom mixture cool slightly, then transfer it to a food processor with the almonds and pecans. Pulse, pausing to scrape down the bowl as needed, until the filling is well combined and has a smooth texture. Set aside in a covered bowl.

2. In a large pot fitted with a steamer insert, add 2 cups water. Place the cabbage leaves in the steamer until they are soft, about 5 minutes. Gently remove the leaves from the steamer and set them aside to cool and drain.

3. To make the sauce, in a large skillet over low heat, sauté the onion in the olive oil until it softens, about 10 minutes. Add the chardonnay, increase the heat, and bring to a boil. Reduce the heat to a simmer and cook until only ½ cup of the wine remains, about 10 minutes. Add the vegetable stock, tomato paste, evaporated cane juice, herbes de Provence, and salt. Season to taste with pepper. Let the sauce simmer for about 20 minutes, or until reduced by a third and slightly thickened. Meanwhile, begin assembling the cabbage rolls.

4. Preheat the oven to 350 degrees F.

5. To assemble the rolls, place about ½ cup of filling near the bottom (stem end) of each cabbage leaf. Fold the bottom of the cabbage leaf over the stuffing and in toward the center; holding in the left and right sides of the leaf, roll up the leaf like a package. Place stuffed cabbage leaves seam side down in a large rectangular baking dish. Pour the sauce over the top of the cabbage leaves and bake, covered with foil, for 30 minutes, or until cabbage leaves are very soft and the filling is piping hot. Be sure to serve up all of the sauce, spooning it on top of each cabbage roll.

Carrot Tzimmes

This warming stew is most popular on Rosh Hashanah, as its sweetness symbolizes the hopes and promise of the new year. I've included it here because it is also often served as a side dish at Passover—though it's so good, I expect to make it throughout the year.

1 small onion, diced

2 cloves garlic, crushed

2 tablespoons extra-virgin olive oil

1 rib celery, cut into 1-inch pieces

4 large carrots, peeled and cut into ½-inch chunks

1 medium yam, peeled and cubed

2 medium sweet potatoes, peeled and cubed

10 pitted prunes, quartered

2 tablespoons maple syrup

1 medium apple, peeled, cored, and cubed

½ teaspoon sea salt

½ teaspoon freshly ground pepper

½ teaspoon ground cinnamon

1¼ cups orange juice

1. In a large stockpot over low heat, sauté the onion and garlic in the olive oil until they are just beginning to brown, about 10 minutes. Add the celery and carrots, and continue cooking, stirring as the carrots soften, for 10 minutes. Add the yam, sweet potatoes, prunes, maple syrup, apple, salt, pepper, and cinnamon. Add the orange juice and stir to combine.

2. Cover the pot with a tight-fitting lid and simmer, stirring periodically, for about 1 hour, or until all the vegetables are soft.

Fresh Fruit Tart

A jaw dropper! This tart looks like the beauties you see in Parisian patisseries beckoning you to take pleasure in a luxurious slice on a spring evening. The instructions look lengthy and intensive, but the process is actually fairly simple and will build confidence, as I am certain your end result will be spectacular.

FOR THE CRUST:

⅓ cup coconut oil

1 cup sorghum flour

¼ teaspoon sea salt

½ teaspoon vanilla extract

1 tablespoon maple syrup

FOR THE CUSTARD:

½ cup cashew butter (I like to use raw cashew butter)

1 tablespoon maple syrup

Zest of 1 medium orange (about 2 tablespoons)

Juice of ½ medium lemon (about 1½ tablespoons)

1 teaspoon vanilla extract

Pinch of salt

FOR THE TOPPING:

1 pint (2 cups) strawberries

1 cup blueberries

1 tablespoon apricot jam

1 tablespoon water

1. Preheat the oven to 350 degrees F.

2. To make the tart crust, set up a stand mixer fitted with the paddle attachment. Add all the crust ingredients and mix until they are just combined; the dough will look like little pearls. Using your hands, press the crumbly dough into a 9-inch tart pan with a removable bottom. (Do not use a rolling pin.) The crust will be very thin; the base should be the thinnest, with the sides a little bit more substantial. Bake for 15 minutes, or until golden. Remove from the oven. If the sides have slumped during baking, just push them gently back into place while the crust is still warm. Let cool.

3. To make the custard, combine all the ingredients in the cleaned stand mixer bowl fitted with the paddle attachment and whip on high speed until thick and creamy. You may need to scrape the bowl with your spatula a few times between beatings to ensure that all the ingredients have been thoroughly incorporated.

4. To make the topping, rinse the strawberries and blueberries and pat dry. Create a flat base on each strawberry by cutting off the stem.

5. In a small saucepan over low heat, combine the apricot jam and water. Heat until a thin syrup forms and just starts to bubble.

6. To assemble the tart, spoon the custard onto the crust and gently spread with a spatula to cover evenly. Arrange the strawberries (cut side down) and blueberries atop the custard. With a small pastry brush, gently brush apricot glaze onto the berries. Remove the rim of the tart pan but keep the base in place to easily transfer the tart to a serving platter. Serve immediately or chill, lightly covered, up to two days in the refrigerator.

MENU

Creamy Lima Bean Soup

Fresh Pea Shoot Salad

Steamed Greens and Polenta with
Shiitake Walnut Sauce

Seedy Baguettes

Coconut Dream Cake

Dark Chocolate Brownies

Cookie-Cutter Vanilla Cookies (page 44),
in the shape of eggs and bunnies

SERVES 6

EASTER

WITH THE ONSET OF SPRING, budding trees, and brighter days, comes the desire for dazzling flavor and the joy of celebrating new life. Whenever I recall holiday memories, my mind is full of color. Easter conjures up fluffy white bunnies, pale yellow chicks, vivid yellow and orange daffodils, cheerily painted cookies in soft blues and pinks, and, of course, the rich browns of chocolate. This imagery greatly influences the flavors I bring to life in these celebration meals.

This Easter menu contains both lively and delicate flavors. To make your Easter day more relaxing, many parts of this menu may be prepared ahead. The coconut cake can be made the day before, as can the polenta, up to the point before it is fried. The mushroom sauce may be made a day or two in advance and warmed before topping your bed of greens and polenta. The baguette will be tastiest when it is made the same day it is to be eaten. The salad is, of course, best made just before serving. I always recommend involving the whole family with cooking and baking, but this is particularly true of the cookie-cutter cookies. Little cookies in the shapes of bunnies, eggs, chicks, and flowers are such a treat to decorate with colored frosting.

I hope your Easter is filled with egg hunts, time spent in the garden, and the company of family and friends over a lovely supper.

Creamy Lima Bean Soup

This fresh lima bean soup is mild, smooth, and flavorful. I find it to be just the right introduction to the polenta entrée with its more intense semblance. Fresh baby lima beans are such a specialty, and their return each spring is something I love to celebrate.

¼ cup olive oil

2 cups chopped leeks (about 2 leeks)

4 cups freshly shelled baby lima beans

5 cups vegetable stock

2 tablespoons freshly squeezed lemon juice

¾ teaspoon sea salt

¼ teaspoon freshly ground pepper

½ cup thinly sliced green onions

1. In a large soup pot over medium heat, sauté the leeks in the olive oil for 8 minutes, or until tender. Add the lima beans and vegetable stock and bring to a boil. Reduce the heat and simmer for about 12 minutes, or until the beans are soft.

2. Carefully transfer the soup to a blender or food processor and puree in two or three batches until a smooth consistency is achieved. Once all of the soup has been pureed, stir in the lemon juice, salt, and pepper. Divide the soup among 6 bowls and top with green onions.

Fresh Pea Shoot Salad

This salad of fresh green tendrils is one that I make many times throughout the spring. It is very bright, tasty, and full of nourishment. You should be able to purchase pea vines at your local farmers market, but if you can't find any, feel free to substitute with mâche, watercress, arugula, or mixed baby lettuces.

Juice of 1 medium lemon (about 3 tablespoons)

3 tablespoons extra-virgin olive oil

⅛ teaspoon evaporated cane juice

½ teaspoon sea salt

Freshly ground pepper

1 pound pea vines, or ½ pound baby lettuce

½ pound radishes (about 10 medium), very thinly sliced

1 medium apple, peeled, cored, and very thinly sliced

1 tablespoon fresh lemon thyme, finely chopped

½ cup finely chopped toasted walnuts

1. In a small bowl, whisk together the lemon juice, olive oil, evaporated cane juice, and salt. Season to taste with pepper and set aside.

2. Prepare the pea vines by removing the leaves and tendrils from the heavier stems. Discard the stems and chop the tendrils into bite-size pieces. In a large bowl, combine the pea vines, radishes, apple, and lemon thyme. Toss well with the dressing and serve topped with the walnuts.

Steamed Greens and Polenta with Shiitake Walnut Sauce

I've been a fan of polenta since I was a very little girl. I used to request fried polenta for every birthday breakfast! This is a deliciously rich entrée with a sauce reminiscent of an Alfredo.

FOR THE SAUCE:

> 2 cups (about 4 ounces) dried shiitake mushrooms
>
> 4½ cups boiling water
>
> 1 cup sun-dried tomatoes (not oil-packed)
>
> 1 cup walnuts
>
> 3 cloves garlic
>
> 1 teaspoon sea salt
>
> ½ teaspoon dried sage
>
> ½ teaspoon herbes de Provence
>
> 1 tablespoon extra-virgin olive oil

FOR THE POLENTA:

> 3 cups water
>
> 1 teaspoon sea salt
>
> 1 cup quick-cooking polenta
>
> Extra-virgin olive oil, for frying the polenta

FOR THE GREENS:

> 2 bunches of your favorite dark, leafy greens, stems removed, greens chopped
>
> 3 tablespoons extra-virgin olive oil
>
> Pinch of sea salt

1. Begin making the sauce by soaking the dried shiitake mushrooms in 1½ cups of the boiling water for 30 minutes. In a separate bowl, soak the sun-dried tomatoes in the remaining 3 cups boiling water. While they are reconstituting, prepare the polenta.

2. To make the polenta, in a medium saucepan, add the water and salt, and bring to a boil. Slowly stir in the polenta. Reduce the heat to a simmer and continue stirring until the polenta thickens and is firm enough to be poured out onto a cutting board to set. (The amount of time will vary depending on the type of polenta you use—follow package instructions.) With wet hands, shape the polenta into a 1-inch-thick rectangle and let set while you finish the sauce.

3. Strain the sun-dried tomatoes and shiitake mushrooms, reserving the mushroom soaking liquid and discarding the tomato liquid. Trim away and discard the tough shiitake stems. Set the tomatoes and mushrooms aside in separate bowls. In a blender, combine the reserved mushroom liquid, walnuts, garlic, salt, sage, and herbes de Provence and thoroughly purée. In a medium skillet over medium heat, sauté the shiitake mushrooms in the olive oil until browned, about 10 minutes. Add the puréed sauce and sun-dried tomatoes. Keep the sauce warm as you prepare the greens.

4. In a large pot fitted with a steamer insert, bring 2 cups water to a boil. Place the greens in the steamer and toss them with the olive oil and salt. Steam the greens until they are tender, about 5 minutes. Drain the greens in a colander and set aside.

5. Cut the polenta rectangle into 6 even rectangles, then cut each of these diagonally to make 12 wedges. In a large skillet over medium heat, working in batches, fry the polenta wedges in the olive oil on both sides until crisp, about 3 minutes per side. Keep the polenta warm in the oven as you work through the batches.

6. To assemble the dish, on each plate place a polenta wedge, then a layer of greens and sauce; top with another polenta wedge and more sauce.

Seedy Baguettes

Doesn't a baguette go with just about any meal? I love to slice it down the center and lather it with succulent spreads, or use it to soak up my salad dressing or last spoonfuls of soup. I continue to approach my gluten-free bread recipes with a commitment to using whole grain flours. Due to the absence of starches, you will find the breads in this cookbook to be heavier, but so nutritious and tasty. This chewy baguette is bound to be a favorite in your household.

2 tablespoons chia seeds

⅓ cup water

1 tablespoon active dry yeast

1¼ cups lukewarm water

2 tablespoons maple syrup

1 tablespoon extra-virgin olive oil

1 cup teff flour

1 cup brown rice flour, plus extra for dusting

½ cup coconut flour

½ cup cornmeal, plus extra for coating loaves

1 teaspoon sea salt, plus extra for sprinkling loaves

2 tablespoons sesame seeds, for coating loaves

1 tablespoon flaxseeds, for coating loaves

1. Begin by soaking the chia seeds in the ⅓ cup water for at least 15 minutes. Preheat the oven to 350 degrees F and generously dust your work surface with brown rice flour.

2. In a large mixing bowl, dissolve the yeast in the lukewarm water. Add the maple syrup and olive oil, and as the yeast begins to foam and feed on the

maple syrup, add the teff, brown rice, and coconut flours; cornmeal; salt; and chia seeds with their soaking liquid. Mix until a soft dough forms.

3. Divide the dough into two sections. Form each into a 12-inch snake shape. Coat the unbaked baguettes abundantly with the sesame seeds and flaxseeds and extra cornmeal. Place the loaves in a baguette pan or on a baking sheet and, with a sharp knife, score lengthwise down the center of both loaves. Sprinkle with additional salt and bake for 1 hour and 10 minutes, or until golden and firm.

Coconut Dream Cake

The title is accurate: all you coconut lovers will find this dreamy and delectable. It's a perfect white cake for the spring season. Note that this recipe as written makes a single-layer cake, but the ingredients can easily be doubled to create a multi-layer cake.

FOR THE CAKE:

> ½ cup canola or extra-virgin olive oil
>
> 1 cup canned unsweetened coconut milk
>
> 2 teaspoons vanilla extract
>
> 1 cup maple syrup
>
> 2½ cups brown rice flour
>
> 1½ teaspoons baking soda
>
> 1 teaspoon sea salt
>
> 1 cup unsweetened shredded coconut

FOR THE FROSTING:

> 1 cup coconut oil
>
> 2 cups powdered evaporated cane juice
>
> ¼ teaspoon sea salt
>
> 2 teaspoons vanilla extract
>
> 1 cup toasted unsweetened shredded coconut
>
> Toasted coconut flakes or shaved dark chocolate curls, for garnish (optional)

1. To make the cake, preheat the oven to 350 degrees F and lightly grease a 9-inch cake pan.

2. In a large mixing bowl, combine the canola oil, coconut milk, vanilla, and maple syrup. In a separate bowl, combine the flour, baking soda, salt, and coconut.

Whisk the dry ingredients into the wet ingredients and thoroughly combine. Pour the batter into the pan and bake for 55 minutes, or until a toothpick inserted into the center comes out clean.

3. To make the frosting, in the bowl of a stand mixer fitted with the paddle attachment, mix the coconut oil, powdered evaporated cane juice, salt, and vanilla on low speed, until the ingredients are well combined. Then increase the speed to high and whip until the frosting has attained a fluffy, creamy texture. Add the toasted coconut and mix in.

4. Let cake cool completely in the pan. After cooling, transfer the cake to a plate and frost. For extra flair, distribute toasted coconut flakes or chocolate curls over the top of the cake.

Dark Chocolate Brownies

Dark chocolate around Easter is a must! These brownies may serve as a healthier substitute to what is usually brought by the Easter bunny. Coconut flour is perfect for this recipe: it really helps create a fudgy, chewy brownie. For an extra decadent dessert, serve these with your favorite ice cream or sorbet.

8 pitted dried dates

½ cup olive oil

½ cup dark brown sugar

1 teaspoon vanilla extract

½ teaspoon salt

½ teaspoon baking soda

¾ cup cocoa powder

½ cup almond meal

½ cup sorghum flour

½ cup coconut flour

2¾ ounces dark chocolate (72% cacao), finely chopped

1. Begin by simmering the dates in 1 cup water for about 1 hour to soften. This can be done the day before.

2. Preheat the oven to 350 degrees F and grease an 8-inch square baking pan.

3. In a large mixing bowl, combine the olive oil, brown sugar, vanilla, salt, and softened dates with any remaining soaking liquid. In a separate bowl, combine

the baking soda, cocoa powder, almond meal, and flours. Gradually incorporate the dry ingredients into the wet ingredients and stir until well combined. Fold in the chocolate. Pour the batter into the pan and bake for 25 minutes, or until slightly cracking on top. Cut the brownies into 12 squares after cooling.

MENU

....

Green Bean Salad with Tarragon

Cooling Summer Salad

Simple Guacamole

Spicy Stuffed Peppers

Cumin-Scented Corn Bread

Onion Focaccia

Nut Butter Chews

Chocolate Apricot Chunk Cookies

....

Serves 6

Fourth of July

As a young woman, I spent many Independence Days with the man who would become my husband; we rode our bikes right as the grand finale of fireworks was setting off. It was a spectacular feeling cycling under the grandeur of light, color, and sound as the audience oohed and aahed, and car horns beeped in celebration.

Now my family heads down to a nearby lake to watch the fireworks. We bring the picnic items that follow. This menu is full of summer flavors with a little extra oomph in anticipation of a long evening spent outdoors in the cool air as the sun goes down and the fireworks begin.

A few tips for transporting this moveable feast: The guacamole will keep its beautiful bright green color if you keep an avocado pit in the container. To keep the stuffed peppers warm, pack them individually in foil and place them snuggly side by side in your picnic basket. Similarly, wrap the cornbread in foil to keep it warm. The rest of the menu is a snap to pack. Happy Fourth of July!

Green Bean Salad
with Tarragon

Just the right ratio of soft pink onion to bright green beans, combined with zesty lemon and a hint of tarragon makes my mouth water. This is a perfect picnic salad in that it can be made hours ahead of time, and the longer it marinates, the tastier it becomes.

½ medium red onion, sliced into paper-thin half moons

Zest of 1 medium lemon (about 2 teaspoons)

¼ cup chopped fresh tarragon leaves

⅓ cup extra-virgin olive oil

Juice of ½ medium lemon (about 1½ tablespoons)

One 15-ounce can cannellini beans, rinsed and drained

1½ pounds green beans, trimmed

1 teaspoon sea salt

Freshly ground pepper

1. Bring a large pot of water to a rolling boil. While the water is heating, place the onion, lemon zest, tarragon, olive oil, lemon juice, and cannellini beans in a large bowl. When the water is boiling, add the green beans, cook for 3 minutes, and then strain right away. Add the cooked beans to the other ingredients while they are still warm and toss well. Add the salt and season to taste with pepper.

Cooling Summer Salad

This bright salad comes together quickly. The powerful flavor of oregano and the juicy crunch of fresh corn with zesty lime are like fireworks in my mouth. Fresh corn cut from the cob is a special summer treat and should not be missed!

2 cucumbers

1 pint cherry tomatoes

2 cups fresh cilantro leaves, chopped

Juice of 2 medium limes (about 3 tablespoons)

1 cup fresh corn kernels

¼ cup snipped fresh chives

¼ cup chopped fresh oregano

¼ cup extra-virgin olive oil

1 avocado, chopped

Sea salt and freshly ground pepper

1. Begin by peeling cucumbers so that just a little bit of green skin remains. Dice the cucumbers into quarter-inch pieces and set aside in a large mixing bowl. Wash and halve the tomatoes, adding them to the bowl. Add the cilantro, lime juice, corn, chives, oregano, and olive oil. If you are preparing the salad in advance, wait to add the avocado until right before serving. Season to taste with salt and pepper.

Simple Guacamole

Let's face it: there's no need to reinvent the wheel when it comes to guacamole. Although there are many variations, I prefer a more traditional guacamole with just a few ingredients.

2 avocados, pitted and peeled (reserve one pit for storing the guacamole)

Juice of 1 medium lime (about 1½ tablespoons)

2 cloves garlic

1½ teaspoons sea salt

3 tablespoons chopped fresh cilantro

1. Using a mortar and pestle or a bowl and wooden spoon, combine the avocados, lime juice, garlic, and salt. Mash well until the ingredients are thoroughly mixed and the guacamole is fairly smooth but still a little lumpy. Stir in the chopped cilantro. If you are making the guacamole in advance, store it in an airtight container in the refrigerator with the reserved avocado pit.

Spicy Stuffed Peppers

These stuffed peppers have a fair amount of heat. If you prefer a milder taste, use just half of the green chile or omit it altogether. This recipe comes together with ease but gives the impression of something more elaborate. The accompaniment of creamy, cooling guacamole (see page 125) is a must.

3 red bell peppers, halved, ribs and seeds discarded

2 shallots, minced

1 tablespoon extra-virgin olive oil

1 green chile, seeded and minced

1 teaspoon chili powder

½ cup fresh or frozen corn (thawed, if frozen)

1½ cups cooked black beans

½ teaspoon sea salt

¼ cup chopped fresh cilantro, for garnish

¼ cup chopped fresh oregano, for garnish

1. Preheat the oven to 350 degrees F.

2. In a baking dish, bake the bell pepper halves cut side up for 10 minutes, or until they are soft. While the peppers are baking, prepare the filling. In a large skillet over low heat, sauté the shallots in the olive oil until they just begin to brown, about 10 minutes. Add the chile and chili powder and cook for about 1 minute before adding the corn, beans, and salt. Cook, stirring, for about 5 minutes.

3. Divide the filling among the peppers. Cover the dish with aluminum foil and bake for an additional 10 minutes. Serve garnished with cilantro and oregano.

Cumin-Scented Corn Bread

Two ingredients make this corn bread especially good: sweet sautéed onions and toasted cumin seeds. This bread is best served just after it has cooled enough to slice, but while it is still warm.

3 tablespoons chia seeds

½ cup water

1 medium onion, diced

1 teaspoon cumin seeds, toasted in a dry pan until fragrant

1 tablespoon extra-virgin olive oil

1 cup teff flour

1 cup cornmeal

2 teaspoons baking powder

½ teaspoon sea salt

¼ cup extra-virgin olive oil

1 tablespoon maple syrup

1. Soak the chia seeds in the water. Preheat the oven to 350 degrees F and lightly grease an 8-inch square baking pan.

2. In a medium skillet, sauté the onion and cumin seeds in the olive oil until the onions are translucent and beginning to brown, about 10 minutes. Set aside to cool.

3. In a medium bowl, combine the teff flour, cornmeal, baking powder, and salt. In a separate large bowl, combine the olive oil, maple syrup, and chia seeds with their soaking liquid. Thoroughly incorporate the dry ingredients into the wet ingredients. Fold the onion mixture into the batter. Pour the batter into the pan and bake for 40 minutes, or until golden and firm to the touch.

Onion Focaccia

When my husband had his first bite of this bread, he exclaimed, "What the focaccia?!" My family has been laughing about it ever since. But this focaccia is that good. While some people love the intense, earthy flavor of amaranth flour, others find it too overpowering, so if you are not a fan, simply replace it with another ½ cup teff flour.

2 tablespoons chia seeds

⅔ cup water

1 large yellow onion, thinly sliced into half moons

2 tablespoons olive oil

2 teaspoons herbes de Provence

1 tablespoon active dry yeast

1 cup lukewarm water

1 tablespoon maple syrup

1 cup brown rice flour

1½ cups teff flour

½ cup amaranth flour

1 teaspoon salt

1. Begin by soaking the chia seeds in the ⅔ cup water for at least 15 minutes. Preheat the oven to 350 degrees F.

2. In a medium skillet, sauté the onion with 1 tablespoon of the olive oil and herbes de Provence until the onions begin to brown, about 10 minutes.

3. In a large mixing bowl, dissolve the yeast in the lukewarm water. Add the maple syrup and remaining 1 tablespoon olive oil. When yeast begins to foam, mix in the flours and salt. Stirring continuously, add the chia seeds with their soaking liquid. Mix until a soft dough forms. Knead the dough gently and shape into a rectangle roughly 9 by 13 inches. Place on a baking sheet. Spread the onions over the dough. Sprinkle with additional salt and bake for 1 hour, or until golden and firm.

Nut Butter Chews

A picnic favorite! These are rich but not overly sweet, and the coconut flour keeps the cookies very soft. I like to use dark chocolate with 85 percent cacao in this recipe, but by all means, if you prefer sweeter chocolate, there is no need to hold back.

½ cup coconut oil

½ cup peanut butter or almond butter

1 teaspoon vanilla extract

⅔ cup packed dark brown sugar

1 teaspoon sea salt

2 cups coconut flour

2 cups water

1 cup chopped walnuts

5½ ounces dark chocolate (85% cacao), coarsely chopped

1. Preheat the oven to 350 degrees F and lightly grease 2 cookie sheets.

2. In a large mixing bowl, cream together the coconut oil, peanut butter, vanilla, brown sugar, and salt using an electric mixer on low speed. Add the coconut flour and water, mixing well to form a soft dough. Fold in the walnuts and chocolate. Roll the dough between your palms to form 1-inch balls (you should have about 20) and transfer to the cookie sheets. Press each ball with the back of a fork to make a crosshatch pattern; if the dough is sticking, dip your fork in a little coconut flour. Bake for 12 minutes, or until golden.

Chocolate Apricot Chunk Cookies

Growing up in Seattle, I used to frequent a wonderful bakery called Macrina Bakery and Cafe. I remember thoroughly enjoying Macrina's chocolate apricot cookies. Here is my gluten-free, vegan version, abundant with gooey dark chocolate.

½ cup extra-virgin olive oil

½ cup Sucanat

1 teaspoon vanilla extract

2 cups teff flour

½ teaspoon baking powder

¼ teaspoon sea salt

1 teaspoon ground cinnamon

½ cup water

¾ cup dried Turkish apricots, thinly sliced

5½ ounces dark chocolate (72% cacao), coarsely chopped

1. Preheat the oven to 350 degrees F and lightly grease 2 cookie sheets.

2. In the bowl of a stand mixer fitted with the paddle attachment, thoroughly combine the olive oil, Sucanat, and vanilla. Add the teff flour, baking powder, salt, cinnamon, and water, mixing at medium speed to form a smooth dough. Remove the bowl from the mixer and fold in the apricots and chocolate by hand. Roll the dough between your palms to form 1½-inch balls and transfer to the cookie sheets. Gently flatten the balls with the palm of your hand. Bake for 15 minutes, or until golden.

MENU

Witch's Pumpkin Brew Stew

Scarily Delicious Green Salad

Lilli's Spooky, Spicy Garbanzos

Yam Bread with a Pinch of Magic

Cookie-Cutter Vanilla Cookies (page 44),
in the shape of ghosts and pumpkins

SERVES 6 TO 8

Halloween

As fall leaves blow in the wind, apples abound, and the sunny but chilly days get shorter, the anticipation of that most mischievous and whimsical of holidays grows. My Halloween menu is full of autumn flavor and spice—much needed before a night of trick-or-treating! The recipes come together with ease. The yam bread is one of the simplest, yet most delicious you will make. I recommend baking it the day it is to be enjoyed. You can make the soup the day before; if you are using fresh pumpkin rather than canned, be sure to allow time for roasting. The cookies can also be made the day before, or you may want to save the Halloween cookie decorating as an activity for family and friends to enjoy.

Years ago a little girl came into the Flying Apron Bakery dressed up for Halloween. She was all in pink: a pink leotard, pink tights, pink feathers. She had taken off her beak, so I was struggling to interpret her costume. Then she stood on one little pink leg and folded her other one up onto her knee. Aha—a flamingo! I hope your Halloween is full of imagination, costumes, and spicy soup spells.

Witch's Pumpkin Brew Stew

This Halloween harvest soup is so scrumptious and aromatic, it just might wake the dead! In this recipe I call for sweetening the pot with a hint of maple syrup. Sometimes I make this soup without any sweetener, and I find the taste to be equally satisfying—so do taste it as you go, adjusting the maple syrup amount to meet your culinary desires.

    2 medium yellow onions, chopped
    2 cloves garlic, minced
    3 tablespoons extra-virgin olive oil
    ⅛ teaspoon red pepper flakes
    1 tablespoon curry powder
    ½ teaspoon ground coriander
    Three 15-ounce cans pumpkin, or 6 cups mashed cooked fresh pumpkin
    5 cups vegetable broth
    Two 15-ounce cans unsweetened coconut milk
    Up to ¼ cup maple syrup
    Sea salt
    Pinch of cayenne (optional)
    ½ cup toasted pumpkin seeds, for garnish

1. In a large saucepan over medium heat, sauté the onions and garlic in the olive oil for about 5 minutes. Add the red pepper flakes, curry powder, and coriander to the pan, and sauté for about 5 more minutes; be sure the spices are well coated with the hot oil. Add the pumpkin and vegetable broth. Stir well and bring the soup to a boil. Reduce the heat and simmer for 15 minutes.

2. Transfer the soup, in batches, to a blender or food processor and blend until smooth. Return the soup to the saucepan. On low heat, add the coconut milk and maple syrup. Adjust the seasonings, adding salt and cayenne to taste.

3. Garnish each bowl of soup with a sprinkle of pumpkin seeds.

Scarily Delicious Green Salad

The name of this dish is no lie—if you have salad lovers partaking in this Halloween feast, you may want to double the recipe. The dressing is so great, almost everyone asks for a second helping.

1 large head red leaf lettuce, torn into bite-size pieces (about 8 cups)

2 heads chicory, stems and center ribs discarded and leaves torn into bite-size pieces (about 8 cups)

⅓ cup extra-virgin olive oil

1½ tablespoons whole grain mustard

1 tablespoon apple cider vinegar

1 teaspoon maple syrup

½ teaspoon sea salt

Freshly ground pepper

⅓ cup finely chopped toasted cashews, for garnish

1. Place the red leaf lettuce and the chicory in a large salad bowl. In a small separate bowl, whisk together the olive oil, mustard, apple cider vinegar, maple syrup, and salt. Season to taste with pepper.

2. Toss the dressing with the greens, coating each leaf. Divide the salad among individual plates and garnish each serving with a sprinkling of cashews.

Lilli's Spooky, Spicy Garbanzos

Indian spices are some of my favorites. I named this recipe for my daughter Lilli, who devours this dish every time I make it. Raisins can replace the currants in a pinch.

1 medium onion, very thinly sliced into half moons

1 tablespoon extra-virgin olive oil

1 teaspoon coriander seeds

1 teaspoon mustard seeds

1 teaspoon curry powder

2 medium tomatoes, chopped (about 2 cups)

2 cups cooked garbanzo beans

¼ cup dried currants

¼ cup chopped cilantro, for garnish

1. In a large skillet over low to medium heat, sauté the onion in the olive oil. When the onion has softened and is beginning to become translucent, about 10 minutes, add the coriander seeds, mustard seeds, and curry powder. As soon as the seeds begin to jump and crackle, 2 to 3 minutes, add the tomatoes and let these cook down for about 5 minutes. Add the garbanzo beans and currants. Simmer, covered, for 1 hour, stirring occasionally. Serve garnished with cilantro.

Yam Bread
with a Pinch of Magic

This recipe comes together in a snap and is sure to please. The hint of coriander in this bread makes for a unique flavor. Enjoy it warm, dipped in olive oil. Should you double the recipe, be sure to form four loaves before baking.

2 cups teff flour, plus extra for kneading

¼ teaspoon baking soda

½ teaspoon sea salt

½ teaspoon ground coriander

¾ cup mashed cooked yam (don't use canned)

⅓ cup water

1. Preheat the oven to 300 degrees F and lightly flour a sheet pan.

2. In a large mixing bowl, or in the bowl of a stand mixer fitted with a dough hook, thoroughly combine the teff flour, baking soda, salt, and coriander. Add the yam, mixing well. Add the water to form a smooth dough. Shape the dough by lightly kneading in additional teff flour until the dough has a smooth surface and a nice coating of flour. Transfer the dough to a lightly floured work surface and form into two narrow 8-inch-long baguettes. Score the loaves lengthwise with a knife about ¼ inch deep. Place loaves on the sheet pan, and bake for 1 hour, or until golden-brown and firm to the touch.

Banana Split Cake

Molasses Spice Cake

Brown Sugar Cake with Blackberry
"Buttercream" Frosting

Orange Almond Cake with Luscious
"Amaretto" Frosting

BIRTHDAY CAKES

PERHAPS THE MOST CELEBRATED HOLIDAYS in my family are our birthdays. Now that I am a mom, I have to say that my daughter's birthday is the most special day of all! The cakes that follow will conclude any birthday meal with style. I love them for many reasons, but mostly because they are completely satisfying without being overly sweet. (For a toddler or a baby's first birthday, the cakes are scrumptious even served without the frosting.) Placing them on a beautiful cake pedestal enhances their festive look. I find this quote an apt description of birthday festivities: "A simple celebration, a gathering of friends; here is wishing you great happiness, a joy that never ends." May your celebrations be filled with merriment!

Banana Split Cake

This was my daughter's first birthday cake. The ever-so-rich banana cake with dark chocolate frosting and mouthwatering, gooey date-pecan filling is a birthday gift in itself.

MAKES ONE 9-INCH, TWO-LAYER CAKE

FOR THE FILLING:

> 1 pound pitted dates, roughly chopped
>
> 1½ cups water
>
> 2 cups lightly toasted pecan halves, plus another 10 pecan halves for decorating the cake
>
> Pinch of salt

FOR THE FROSTING:

> 5½ ounces dark baking chocolate (72% cacao), finely chopped
>
> ⅓ cup coconut oil
>
> ½ cup water
>
> 1 teaspoon vanilla extract
>
> Pinch of salt

FOR THE CAKE:

> ½ cup canola or extra-virgin olive oil
>
> 1 cup canned unsweetened coconut milk
>
> 2 teaspoons vanilla extract
>
> 1 cup maple syrup
>
> 2 medium bananas, mashed
>
> 2½ cups brown rice flour
>
> 1½ teaspoons baking soda
>
> 1 teaspoon sea salt

1. Begin by starting the filling. Place the dates and water in a large saucepan over low heat and simmer for 1 hour, stirring occasionally, until the dates are quite soft. Be sure the liquid does not completely evaporate.

2. While the dates cook, begin making the frosting. In a double boiler or using a metal bowl set over a saucepan of simmering water, melt the chocolate with the coconut oil. When all the chocolate has melted, whisk in the water, vanilla, and salt. Refrigerate the frosting for 1 hour, taking it out and whisking occasionally.

3. While the frosting sets, make the cake. Preheat the oven to 350 degrees F and lightly grease two 9-inch cake pans.

4. In a large mixing bowl or the bowl of a stand mixer fitted with the paddle attachment, combine the canola oil, coconut milk, vanilla, maple syrup, and bananas. In a separate bowl, combine the brown rice flour, baking soda, and salt. Gradually incorporate the dry ingredients into the wet ingredients, mixing thoroughly. Divide batter equally between the two cake pans. Bake for 30 minutes, or until the cakes spring back when you press the center with your finger and a toothpick inserted into the middle comes out clean. Allow the cakes to cool completely before removing from the pan and assembling.

5. While the cakes cool, finish making the filling. Drain the dates and pulse in a food processor until they have a smooth consistency. Transfer the date paste to a separate bowl, clean the processor, and add the pecans and salt. Pulse until a creamy nut butter forms.

6. To assemble, place one cake layer on a platter and using a cake spatula or butter knife, spread the pecan butter on it. Atop the pecan butter spread about 1 cup of the date paste. Place the second cake layer atop the first and spread the remaining date paste on it. Finally, spread the chocolate frosting over the date filling; cover the sides of the cake as well. (If the frosting has become too solid after refrigeration, try spreading it with a heated knife, or heat frosting slightly and whip in a stand mixer until it is spreadable.) For an extra-nice presentation, place pecan halves in a circle around the top of the cake.

Molasses Spice Cake

This prize-winning cake is a perfect balance of moistness and delicate texture, with a velvety, rich flavor that hints of molasses. You will notice I call for gluten-free oat flour, which I believe is a key ingredient in the amazing texture of this cake. If you are having difficulty finding gluten-free oat flour in your area, you can substitute rice flour or, perhaps, mill your own using gluten-free oats, which are now becoming more widely available.

MAKES ONE 9-INCH, TWO-LAYER CAKE OR TWENTY 2¾-INCH CUPCAKES

FOR THE CAKE:

⅔ cup extra-virgin olive oil or canola oil

1½ cups water

¾ cup maple syrup

½ cup molasses

1 cup gluten-free oat flour

2 cups brown rice flour

2 teaspoons baking soda

½ teaspoon sea salt

¼ teaspoon ground cloves

1 teaspoon ground cinnamon

FOR THE FROSTING:

1 cup coconut oil

1 cup powdered evaporated cane juice

2 tablespoons molasses

¼ teaspoon sea salt

1. To make the cake, preheat the oven to 350 degrees F and lightly grease two 9-inch cake pans or line two 2¾-inch cupcake pans with paper liners.

2. In a large mixing bowl or the bowl of a stand mixer fitted with the paddle attachment, combine the olive oil, water, maple syrup, and molasses. In a separate bowl, combine the oat and brown rice flours, baking soda, salt, cloves, and cinnamon. Gradually incorporate the dry ingredients into the wet ingredients, mixing thoroughly. Divide batter equally between the two cake pans or about 20 cupcake tins. Bake cakes for 45 minutes, or until they spring back when you press the center with your finger. Bake cupcakes for 25 minutes, or until a toothpick inserted in the center comes out clean. Allow the cakes to cool completely before frosting.

3. While the cakes cool, make the frosting. (Note: If you are baking cupcakes and plan to pipe on the frosting, I recommend doubling the frosting recipe so you have plenty to work with in your piping bag.) In a large mixing bowl, add all the ingredients and beat with an electric mixer on low speed until combined. Increase the speed to high and whip until the frosting is smooth and creamy. You may need to scrape down the sides of the bowl a few times to be sure all the ingredients are incorporated.

4. To assemble, place one cake layer on a platter and, using a cake spatula or butter knife, spread with a small portion of frosting. Place the second layer on top of the first, and with the remaining frosting, cover the top and sides of the cake. Frost cupcakes with a butter knife, or pipe frosting on for a fancier look.

Brown Sugar Cake with Blackberry "Buttercream" Frosting

I developed this recipe with my dear sister, Jules, while on a sunny winter walk. The more we walked, the more our appetites increased. Being pregnant and craving very specific flavors, Jules felt adamant about this combination of a brown sugar cake with a "buttery" frosting containing fresh blackberries. I have to say, it is brilliant! And the frosting is a beautiful magenta hue.

MAKES ONE 9-INCH, TWO-LAYER CAKE OR TWENTY 2¾-INCH CUPCAKES

FOR THE CAKE:

⅔ cup extra-virgin olive oil or canola oil

1½ cups water

1⅓ cups packed dark brown sugar

1 teaspoon vanilla extract

3 cups brown rice flour

2 teaspoons baking soda

½ teaspoon sea salt

FOR THE FROSTING:

1 cup coconut oil

2 cups powdered evaporated cane juice

2 teaspoons vanilla extract

¼ teaspoon sea salt

1 cup fresh blackberries, plus 20 extra for decorating the cake

1. To make the cake, preheat the oven to 350 degrees F and lightly grease two 9-inch cake pans or line two 2¾-inch cupcake pans with paper liners.

2. In a large mixing bowl or the bowl of a stand mixer fitted with the paddle attachment, combine the olive oil, water, brown sugar, and vanilla. In a separate bowl, combine the brown rice flour, baking soda, and salt. Gradually incorporate the dry ingredients into the wet ingredients, mixing thoroughly. Divide batter equally between the two cake pans or about 20 cupcake tins. Bake cakes for 1 hour, or until they spring back when you press the center with your finger. Bake cupcakes for 25 minutes, or until a toothpick inserted in the center comes out clean. Allow the cakes to cool completely before frosting.

3. While the cakes cool, make the frosting. (Note: If you are baking cupcakes and plan to pipe on the frosting, I recommend doubling the frosting recipe so you have plenty to work with in your piping bag.) In a large mixing bowl, add all the ingredients and beat with an electric mixer on low speed until combined. Increase the speed to high and whip until the frosting is smooth and creamy. You may need to scrape down the sides of the bowl a few times to be sure all the ingredients are incorporated.

4. To assemble, place one cake layer on a platter and, using a cake spatula or butter knife, spread with a small portion of frosting. Place the second layer on top of the first, and with the remaining frosting, cover the top and sides of the cake. Frost cupcakes with a butter knife, or pipe frosting on for a fancier look. Place 1 blackberry on top of each cupcake, or arrange them attractively atop the layer cake as a finishing touch.

Orange Almond Cake with Luscious "Amaretto" Frosting

This is a very light cake filled with the texture and sweetness of slivered almonds and a hint of citrus. For extra elegance, some shaved chocolate centered atop the cake provides a lovely accent.

MAKES ONE 9-INCH, TWO-LAYER CAKE OR TWENTY 2¾-INCH CUPCAKES

FOR THE CAKE:

    1 cup extra-virgin olive oil or canola oil

    ½ cup water

    1 cup maple syrup

    2 teaspoons vanilla extract

    1 teaspoon almond extract

    3 cups brown rice flour

    2 teaspoons baking soda

    ½ teaspoon sea salt

    Zest of 1 medium orange (about 2 tablespoons)

    Zest of 1 medium lemon (about 2 teaspoons)

    2 cups slivered almonds

FOR THE FROSTING:

    1 cup coconut oil

    2 cups powdered evaporated cane juice

    ¼ teaspoon sea salt

    1 teaspoon vanilla extract

    ½ teaspoon almond extract

Zest of 1 orange

3 ounces dark chocolate, shaved into curls (optional)

1. To make the cake, preheat the oven to 350 degrees F and lightly grease two 9-inch cake pans or line two 2¾-inch cupcake pans with paper liners.

2. In a large mixing bowl or the bowl of a stand mixer fitted with the paddle attachment, combine the olive oil, water, vanilla and almond extracts, and maple syrup. In a separate bowl, combine the brown rice flour, baking soda, salt, orange and lemon zest, and almonds. Gradually incorporate the dry ingredients into the wet ingredients, mixing thoroughly. Divide batter equally between the two cake pans or about 20 cupcake tins. Bake cakes for 1 hour, or until the cakes spring back when you press the center with your finger. Bake cupcakes for 25 minutes, or until a toothpick inserted in the center comes out clean. Allow the cakes to cool completely before frosting.

3. While the cakes cool, make the frosting. (Note: If you are baking cupcakes and plan to pipe on the frosting, I recommend doubling the frosting recipe so you have plenty to work with in your piping bag.) In a large mixing bowl, add all the ingredients and beat with an electric mixer on low speed until combined. Increase the speed to high and whip until the frosting is smooth and creamy. You may need to scrape down the sides of the bowl a few times to be sure all the ingredients are incorporated.

4. To assemble, place one cake layer on a platter and, using a cake spatula or butter knife, spread with a small portion of frosting. Place the second layer on top of the first, and with the remaining frosting, cover the top and sides of the cake. Frost cupcakes with a butter knife or pipe frosting on for a fancier look. Center the chocolate curls in a circle atop the cake, or place 1 curl on each cupcake.

RESOURCES

**Aunt Patty's Natural Foods
& Ingredients**
www.auntpattys.com
*For canola oil, molasses, brown rice syrup,
nuts, seeds, and agave syrup*

Bob's Red Mill
5000 SE International Way
Milwaukie, OR 97222
800-349-2173
www.bobsredmill.com
*For coconut flour, hazelnut flour, garbanzo
bean flour, fava bean flour, brown rice
flour, yeast, xanthan gum, and many
other gluten-free products*

Dagoba Organic Chocolate
2000 Folsom Street
San Francisco, CA 94110
866-237-0152
www.dagobachocolate.com
For dairy-free dark chocolate chips

Florida Crystals Corporation
1 N Clematis Street, Suite 200
West Palm Beach, FL 33401
877-835-2828
www.floridacrystals.com
For organic whole cane sugar

GloryBee Foods
P.O. Box 2744
Eugene, OR 97402
800-456-7923
www.glorybee.com
*For oils, sweeteners, honey, nuts, seeds,
and nut butters*

Lundberg Family Farms
P.O. Box 369
Richvale, CA 95974
530-882-4551
www.lundberg.com
*For brown rice flour, brown rice syrup,
and rice milk*

Nutiva
P.O. Box 5606
Oxnard, CA 93031
800-993-4367
www.nutiva.com
For chia seeds

Quinoa Corporation
P.O. Box 279
Gardena, CA 90248
310-217-8125
www.quinoa.net
For quinoa flour

Red Star Yeast
P.O. Box 737
Milwaukee, WI 53201
877-677-7000
www.redstaryeast.com
For cake and active dry yeast

Spectrum Naturals
4600 Sleepytime Drive
Boulder, CO 80301
800-434-4246
www.spectrumorganics.com
For palm oil and coconut oil

The Teff Company
888-822-2221
www.teffco.com
For teff flour

INDEX

ABOUT THE AUTHOR

Photo by Rachelle Longé

JENNIFER KATZINGER and her father first opened the doors of the Flying Apron Bakery in 2002, recognizing the value in organic, gluten-free, vegan, and sustainable whole foods years in advance of what has become a rapidly growing industry. After growing the bakery from a tiny take-out window in Seattle's University District to a spacious and lovely café in the city's Fremont neighborhood, Jennifer sold the bakery in 2010, and it continues to thrive.

After selling the bakery, Jennifer pursued her two greatest passions: being a mother, and continuing to develop delicious and healthy recipes. Praise for her first cookbook, *Flying Apron's Gluten-Free & Vegan Baking Book*, inspired her to develop all-new recipes for the home kitchen, centered on holiday themes. Her daughter, one of her greatest joys, was by her side in the kitchen every day, helping or napping, as Jennifer created the menus for this cookbook.

Jennifer earned a BA in English Literature from the University of Washington, and pursued a Master's in Industrial Design from the Pratt Institute in New York City. She lives in Seattle with her husband, Joseph, their daughter, Lillian, and their dog, Neve. They are looking forward to taking Lillian camping in the Pacific Northwest and enjoying beautiful food together.